JAMAICAN VOICEWORKS

23 Traditional and Popular Jamaican Songs

compiled and written by
Michael Burnett and Peter Hunt

series editor: Peter Hunt

MUSIC DEPARTMENT

OXFORD
UNIVERSITY PRESS

OXFORD
UNIVERSITY PRESS

Great Clarendon Street, Oxford OX2 6DP, England
198 Madison Avenue, New York, NY 10016, USA

Oxford University Press is a department of the University of Oxford.
It furthers the University's aim of excellence in research, scholarship,
and education by publishing worldwide in

Oxford New York
Auckland Cape Town Hong Kong Karachi
Kuala Lumpur Madrid Melbourne Mexico City Nairobi
New Delhi Shanghai Taipei Toronto

With offices in

Argentina Austria Brazil Chile Czech Republic France Greece
Guatemala Hungary Italy Japan Poland Portugal Singapore
South Korea Switzerland Thailand Turkey Ukraine Vietnam

Oxford is a registered trade mark of Oxford University Press
in the UK and in certain other countries

© Oxford University Press 2009

Michael Burnett and Peter Hunt have asserted their right under the Copyright,
Designs and Patents Act, 1988, to be identified as the Authors of this Work

Database right Oxford University Press (maker)

First published 2009

ISBN 978–0–19–336050–1

Music and text origination by
Barnes Music Engraving Ltd., East Sussex
Printed in Great Britain on acid-free paper by
Caligraving Ltd., Thetford, Norfolk.

Foreword

The adage 'Every picture tells a story' could be applied to the music of Jamaica, particularly to the folksongs which tell the story of our people. The narration of stories through music, especially songs, was the earliest method for our ancestors to recount their tales in an age devoid of modern technology. Several of these musical stories are embraced in *Jamaican Voiceworks*, including 'You walk an' talk' and 'Mister Potter'. These songs are associated with our traditional way of life, and focus on ceremonies (birth, baptism, and marriage), social gatherings, games, work songs, and mourning.

Although our motto is 'Out of many, one people', 90 per cent of our population comprises people of African descent. Our music has its roots in over 300 years of resistance to slavery and colonial rule, and the consequent fusion of musical styles gives our songs a distinctive and unique sound. As has been argued by folk music experts Miss Lucy Broadwood and Mr C. S. Myers, the tunes of most Jamaican songs derive from Europe, mainly the British Isles, but the rhythms are African in origin, and this blend gives them an essentially Jamaican sound.

I regard this publication as a homage to our ancestors who resisted slavery, and to our wider musical heritage: the Frats Quintet and Louise Bennett, bearers of the traditional folk forms Kumina, mento, and Revival; the Rastafari movement; and Millie Small, Jimmy Cliff, and Bob Marley, the Rastafari movement's famous musical son.

The authors and Oxford University Press must be commended for the publication of *Jamaican Voiceworks*, which is a significant contribution to the intangible heritage of Jamaica's music. Michael Burnett, lecturer at the Jamaica School of Music, Cultural Training Centre (now Edna Manley College of the Visual and Performing Arts), and Peter Hunt, experienced choral director, arranger, and teacher, have created a unique collection, valuable both as a tribute to Jamaica's musical heritage and as an appealing and practical resource book for amateur choirs.

VIVIAN CRAWFORD
Executive Director
Institute of Jamaica

Contents

Except where stated otherwise, the songs in this book are traditional and have been arranged by Michael Burnett, Peter Hunt, and David Blackwell.

Introduction

The award-winning *Voiceworks* handbooks for singing are now firmly established as a resource that encourages those who help other people to sing well and with confidence. Their hallmark is a wide range of accessible material, with teaching notes to guide the leader/conductor/teacher in promoting good practice and technique for enjoyable and healthy singing, for life. The repertoire and arrangements are flexible to cater for unison and part-singing, by voices at all stages of development, and with varying levels of experience.

Jamaican Voiceworks brings this practical approach to singing to the wonderfully rich and varied traditions of the island of Jamaica. As with the *Voiceworks* series, this book has many aims, but the two most important are:

- To introduce teachers, singing leaders, and singers not familiar with the folk and historical traditions of Jamaican culture to a new repertoire, and to encourage them to take a different look at what they already know;
- To share with musicians already familiar with such material some different ways of presenting it through the arrangements here, which make it accessible to a wide range of singers.

The songs give a good insight into the island's culture and history; they either are from Jamaica or, in a few cases, were composed and/or recorded by Jamaican-born musicians. Some are well known, and there are many songs already in regular use; but hopefully this collection also introduces some less familiar material to add to choir repertoires.

Jamaican Voiceworks has five themed sections. Each one contains songs that can be sung in two, three, or four parts, and occasionally up to six parts. Most are accompanied, with options for *a cappella* singing, and most could be sung as solo songs with as much or as little of the vocal backing to suit resources available.

Section I: Dance and Humorous Songs. A selection of songs that explore aspects of Jamaican traditional life and sense of fun.

Section II: Work and Ring-Game Songs. Songs with a practical purpose, in a style for which Jamaica is famous.

Section III: Christmas and Revival Songs. Religious melodies that have been sung by generations of Jamaicans.

Section IV: Rastafarian Songs. Songs drawn from the cult whose beliefs inspired the first reggae musicians.

Section V: Popular Songs. Well-known melodies that are associated with Jamaica by people throughout the world.

See 'Jamaican Song and Dance' for more information about the music of Jamaica.

Apart from these themes, the songs can be grouped according to the following musical criteria:

- **2 parts** Nos. 2, 8, 17
- **3 parts** Nos. 1, 3, 4, 5, 7, 9, 10, 12, 16, 22, 23
- **4 parts** Nos. 6, 11, 14, 18, 19
- **5 parts** Nos. 13, 15, 21
- **6 parts** No. 20
- **Bass clef part for changed voices** Nos. 6, 7, 9, 10, 11, 13, 14, 15, 18, 19, 20, 21, 22, 23
- **Unaccompanied** Nos. 9, 14 (section), 18, 19, 22 (section)
- **Separate instrumental part** Nos. 2, 4, 6, 13
- **Printed percussion parts**: Nos. 5, 18, 19

Throughout the book the expectation is that leaders will prepare their singers for focused work; set the context for each piece; warm up voices; help singers learn in a structured way; interpret each song appropriately; and create a performance given with confidence, purpose, and enjoyment. The supporting notes, in the established *Voiceworks* tradition, help this process, and are identical in structure for each song:

- **You need to know**. The background, and historical and musical context, for each song. This information is essential so that the songs are approached with the right spirit and frame of mind. This knowledge and understanding will help create a meaningful performance with real communication.
- **Warming up**. Detailed exercises to prepare singers for the session in general, and for the particular musical and vocal challenges of each song; and to support learning.
- **Teaching and learning**. A step-by-step guide which breaks down learning into simple stages, making the song accessible to singers and leaders. The implication is that everyone is a learner.
- **Listen out**. Things to be aware of when learning, preparing, and performing. Phrased as questions, they encourage the leader and singers to listen and make their own decisions, with tips to help overcome obstacles.
- **Performing**. Suggestions that relate to the performances on the CD, but with ideas for creating performances to suit the circumstances of each group.

The CD contains performances of all of the songs, and all are recorded complete. They are not concert performances but give a guide to interpretation and cover all vocal parts appearing in the book. In addition, all accompanied songs have a backing track; some of these are recorded with the notated piano accompaniment, but several have been given fuller accompaniments to liven up your performances. Versions of a number of the songs contained in *Jamaican Voiceworks* have been specially recorded for the publication by the mento band The Happy Smilers. The band comes from the Ocho Rios area on the north coast of Jamaica and the recordings give a good idea of the traditional vocal and instrumental sounds of the island. The Happy Smilers use banjo, guitar, and rumba box (see p. x), and their recordings are intended as stylistic illustrations rather than definitive performances of the songs as set out in the book. You will find, for example, that some notes and words differ from the versions published here.

Some general considerations about the music:

- **Arrangements**. The music is presented as a set of arrangements of the original melodies for a variety of voice combinations, but they can be used flexibly to suit your own requirements. Plenty of parts are provided for some songs, to enable larger groups to divide if they wish, but there is no obligation to use them all; virtually all of the songs will work well as solo songs with the written accompaniments, adding as many of the additional parts as desired, depending on the voices and skills available. All of the songs are suitable for younger singers: simply leave out the bass-line and any harmony parts that are not required! The extra vocal lines could of course be performed by instruments. Equally, many songs are flexible in terms of structure, and can be sung through as many times as desired by the group. Where helpful, the supporting notes give suggested performance plans, including details of the song structure used for the backing CD. Except where stated otherwise, the songs in this book are traditional and have been arranged by Michael Burnett, Peter Hunt, and David Blackwell.

- **Musical notation**. The notation is the closest representation of the rhythms to be sung, but of course singers can be flexible, particularly when taking solos. New songs are probably best learnt as written; then, when singers are fully confident, they can be interpreted more loosely and given life of their own.

- **Language**. We have retained some actual Jamaican words and have also included some simple phoneticizations in the notated scores. This is not with the intention or expectation that singers will sound authentically Jamaican, but rather to encourage singers to move away from a very 'English' choral sound, and to get close to a regional dialect. Further/specific pronunciation tips for how to achieve a more colloquial sound in particular songs are given where appropriate in the supporting notes.

- **Voice distribution**. The following labels are used: **Melody**, **Harmony** (mostly **1** & **2**), **Bass**, and **Descant**. Some songs correspond to the more conventional scoring of **Soprano**, **Alto**, and **Baritone** (or **Tenor** and **Bass**), but the more general labels have been used in an effort to encourage choirs to distribute voices across all parts and avoid keeping singers on the same part constantly. This not only gives variety to the songs, but also increases the musical experiences for the singers, and promotes vocal flexibility. Developing and changing male voices (tenors and basses) should sing melody lines—it adds to the texture and helps highlight the melody. Parts in the bass clef are for lower male voices, but all other lines can be taken by any voices. Where particular scoring options are preferable, these are outlined in the supporting notes. Descants are generally optional lines that float above the melody, again adding to variety and texture. These work best, but not exclusively, sung by high voices, and also work well instrumentally. **Mixed voices** means a mixture of voice types on all or most parts.

- **Key and pitch**. Most of the songs are accompanied, but they can be learnt in the early stages, along with the supporting warm ups, in any key that's comfortable. If guitar is used, then transposition is possible using the suggested chords and a capo.

- **Accompaniments**. Originally, if the traditional songs had been accompanied at all, the accompaniments would have been played on instruments such as fife (bamboo flute), harmonica, banjo, and guitar, with possibly a bass instrument such as rumba box (see p. x). Harmonies would have been simple, albeit syncopated, in performance. The piano parts in this collection have been composed to be as simple as possible and to support the singers, while also adding a little original flair and some unexpected harmonies in places to inject a fresh sound and to present them in a way that might appeal to a broad range of listeners. This has been done with respect for the original songs, which have been preserved in the process. Each song has chord symbols for guitar which are generally more basic than some of the piano accompaniments, but remember that nothing is so precious that it can't be altered to suit conditions, provided the integrity of the original melody and words remains intact! Any instrument can be used for the melody, descant, or harmony; the separate instrument parts are played on a flute on the CD, but will work well on a recorder too. The bass-line of the piano, or bass vocal line, could be played on the bass (acoustic or electric), and this would add substantially to the quality of performance. Simple and regular percussion beats—mainly drums of different pitches, and shakers—are typical in indigenous performances and should be encouraged. Always feel free to add any new counter-melodies or other material.

- **Speeds**. Metronome markings are deliberately avoided in order to encourage singers to find a tempo that suits them and the song. The words and musical content should be the guide, along with the CD performances, and tempo and character directions are suggested to help.

- **Dynamics**. Some dynamics are written in, to help shape the music in performance; these are designed to help, but not dictate—use your judgement. Often the dynamic markings given are there to ensure the melody will be heard when other parts are involved.

- **Memory**. Aim to learn the music by heart as soon as possible—this makes for much better singing. None of these songs is very long so it should happen quite quickly. Singing songs little and often helps with this, and young people learn very quickly. Help with visual clues or some physical actions. Remember that there will be a range of learning styles in a singing group (visual, aural, and kinaesthetic), so read, listen, and move!

- **Teaching by rote**. This is the preferred method for teaching and learning songs; it is also good for modelling how you want a group to sing. Teach short phrases one at a time, with as much continuity as possible; don't talk too much, or think aloud. Improve a phrase or pattern by simply repeating it until you hear an improvement. Always praise your singers when they do well, and help them to improve when they don't!

- **Positioning singers**. Consider carefully where to stand singers for rehearsal and performance. A circle is good for practising because it suggests equality and sharing, allows everyone to see and hear each other, and is good for eye contact. It can also make singers feel exposed so judge your group carefully. Mixing up singers completely is good for independence, hearing other parts, and improving choral blend. Grouping in voice parts is the most common, and certainly helps part-learning and aids confidence. Change positions for different pieces in performance—it is visually pleasing as well as vocally rewarding. Actions and some kind of movement appropriate to the song are also good, particularly for young singers.

Jamaican Song and Dance

Jamaican music is, to borrow poet Derek Walcott's phrase, a 'creative synthesis' of African and European musics. The commemoration, in 2007, of the bicentenary of the abolition of the transatlantic slave trade in Africans reminded us of the horrors and scale of the trade. In Jamaica, once the English slavers had expelled the Spanish (in 1655), they attempted to undermine the culture and religion of those they oppressed by, for example, outlawing the use of drums and banning African religious rituals. However, the slaves resisted, retaining fundamental aspects of their African identity, and these have survived until today.

One of the most extraordinary of these retentions is that words of Congolese derivation survive in the religious rituals of the Jamaican Kumina cult, having been passed down from generation to generation, initially under the whip of slavery, and then under the rod of colonialism. Jamaica's slave inheritance is also evident in those African elements which form the basis of the nation's music: the use of call and response structures, of riffs, of syncopated rhythms, of drums and shakers. But the retention of these African elements was not enough for the slaves; for they turned the tables on their oppressors, colonizing their music and breathing African life into their dance tunes, shanties, and hymns.

The Jamaican traditional songs which stem from that creative synthesis form the basis of this book: dance songs, game songs, work songs, and religious songs. But the story of Jamaica's music doesn't end with its rich traditional song repertoire. For, during the 1960s, the island's song and dance tradition gave birth to new, amplified popular music genres—ska, rock steady, and reggae—which brought Jamaica to the attention of the entire musical world. Naturally, this book also contains examples of songs that relate to these genres.

Language

Before discussing the background to the songs, a word about Jamaica's vernacular language is required. The term 'language' is used since the alternatives, 'dialect' or 'patois', seem inadequate when it comes to defining that vibrant re-interpretation of the English tongue through which Jamaicans communicate. We are familiar with aspects of that language through its phoneticization in the lyrics of the nation's popular songs, and in the work of dub-poets such as Linton Kwesi Johnson (see *Selected Poems*, Penguin 2006) and of novelists such as Margaret Cezair-Thompson (*The True History of Paradise*, Headline Review 2009). And it is true that phoneticizing the language can provide the non-Jamaican reader of lyrics, poetry, or a novel with a workable appreciation of it. However, phoneticizing the lyrics of songs for performance by non-Jamaicans poses problems, not least because those performances can sound stilted, even patronizing. So the policy in this book has been a) to use a mixture of simple phoneticizations and actual Jamaican words (the meanings of which are explained), in order to preserve some idea of the language; and b) to avoid phoneticizing everything in the expectation that performers would sound authentically Jamaican. This approach is inevitably a compromise but will work if singers otherwise use vernacular English pronunciation, rather than enunciate vowels and consonants as if members of a well-trained choral society.

☐ Dance and work songs

Jamaica's national dance song—equivalent to the calypso of Trinidad and Tobago but quite distinct from it—is called 'mento'. The words of mento songs, such as No. 4 'Mango Walk', explore issues of relevance to a Jamaican audience, whether social, political, or sexual. Mento tunes use repeated, syncopated rhythms which are less complex, and more dignified, than those of calypso. As well as being sung, mento melodies are played on fife (a bamboo flute) and/or harmonica, accompanied by guitar and/or banjo, rumba box, drums, and a variety of percussion instruments such as coconut-shell graters and spoons. (A rumba box is a large wooden box with sound-hole across which are placed four or five metal strips. The strips are tuned to low-pitched notes of a major scale and are plucked to create a bass-line. The performer sits astride the rumba box.) Guitar and banjo players strum repeated quaver chords as they accompany the melody, placing an emphasis on the fourth beat of each 4/4 bar.

Just as mento melodies are performed instrumentally, so tunes from quadrille dancing have often become songs. The quadrille (pronounced 'catreel' in Jamaican) dates back to slavery when dances from Europe, such as the reel, waltz, polka, and mazurka, were brought to Jamaica by the plantation owners. The dances, or figures, were grouped in sets of five and played at the estate houses on imported instruments such as flute, violin, and piano. Eventually, quadrille bands were formed by slaves using instruments such as those mentioned in relation to mento. No. 2 'Run, Moses, run' and No. 5 'Fan me soldier man' are quadrille melodies.

Jonkunnu (see 'Horsehead', p. xiv) is a song and dance form which stems from the African Ashanti tradition and is associated with Christmas celebrations in Jamaica. Drumming, using double-headed keg drums and sometimes a bass drum, dominates Jonkunnu music-making. Dance melodies are played on fifes and a variety of other percussion instruments are also used.

'Brown Girl in the Ring' (No. 10) is the most famous of Jamaican children's ring-game songs. The simple structure and lyrics, and repetitive rhythms, of such songs make them memorable and therefore well suited to their purpose, which is to facilitate the playing of the related game. The stylized 'motions' associated with the games do, of course, make them dances of a kind, and hand-clapping is often used to create dramatic and percussive effect. Details of the game/dance associated with 'Brown Girl in the Ring' are on page 38, and of another game song, No. 8 'Jane an' Louisa', on page 32. 'Jane an' Louisa' is one of the songs that were introduced by English missionaries when they set up schools for Jamaican children after emancipation. Subsequently the melodies and rhythms of these songs have been adapted, and their themes, language, and movement transformed, in order to give them a thoroughly Jamaican identity.

Work songs were used during and after slavery as a means of coordinating the actions of a gang of labourers as they worked on the plantation, railway line, or banana wharf (see No. 11 'Day da light'). The labourers sang as they worked, responding, often using improvised harmonies, to the short melodic phrases declaimed by the leader of the group (the 'bomma man'), and moving to the slow beat of the music. This kind of solo–chorus song structure is an example of call and response patterning.

☐ Religious songs

Religion has always played an important part in Jamaican life, and Revivalism has its origins in the 'Great Revival' of the 1860s, when English preachers enthused their Jamaican audiences with dramatic re-tellings of biblical stories. Two Revivalist sects—Revival Zion and

Pocomania—survive today. Their ceremonies feature lively hymn-singing (see No. 12 'Wash an' be Clean'), accompanied by drums, rattles, and cymbals, and by hand-clapping. Improvised harmonies are often added to the hymns, and the ceremonies also feature 'trumping' (or 'trooping'), a form of vocalized deep breathing to a regular beat. These Revivalist ceremonies well demonstrate the African–European creative synthesis: much of the ritual is of African origin, yet the hymn tunes stem from the English tradition.

Rastafarianism (see Section IV) developed in Jamaica during the 1930s. The cult partly derived its scriptures and beliefs from the Bible and Christianity, and subsequently became the religious force behind the first reggae songs forty years later. Drumming is fundamental to Rastafarian songs and ritual, with three drums being used: the high-pitched repeater; the medium-pitched fundeh; and the bass drum, which dominates all that goes on with its repeated quavers on the first beat of each bar. Rastafarians believe that Ethiopia is their spiritual homeland and their songs often refer to this belief.

From ska to reggae

Reggae music emerged at the end of the 1960s after a decade of exciting developments in Jamaican amplified popular music. The decade began with ska, whose pronounced bass-lines, busy off-beat quavers, and, initially at least, serious lyrics, confirm it to be an off-shoot of mento. Indeed, Bob Marley's first hit, 'Simmer down', is a classic ska recording which demonstrates the influence of the mento songs he heard during his childhood in the rural parish of St Ann.

Ska was followed, in about 1965, by rock steady. Rock steady initially had much in common with ska, but its slower tempo enabled the development of more complex melodic lines and lyrics, and made its off-beat chords more deliberate. However, rock steady soon became most clearly defined by its heavily emphasized bass guitar riffs.

Reggae adopted an even slower tempo than rock steady but retained its riffs and maintained its off-beat emphasis by placing repeated quaver chords on the second and fourth beats of songs. Reggae riffs tend to be less busy than those of rock steady, with rests often occurring on strong beats, giving those beats a silent emphasis which is unique to reggae (and also to reggae dance, when dancers move just after strong beats as if being struck by them). The last section of this book contains examples of ska-related and reggae songs.

Acknowledgements

Michael would like to express warm thanks to Vivian Crawford for contributing the foreword and allowing access to his extensive knowledge of Jamaican traditional music and culture, and to John Morgan for facilitating the song recordings by The Happy Smilers Mento Band.

Peter would like to thank Rebecca Berkeley for her contribution to research and teaching notes, as well as for rehearsing the CD singers.

The authors would also like to express their deep gratitude to Mary Chandler from OUP for her commitment and skilled dedication to this project, and her kind assistance in editing and production; also to David Blackwell for his guidance throughout.

Preparing to Sing

It is **absolutely vital** that singers prepare their bodies and voices for a singing rehearsal in the same way that an athlete prepares for activity. This focuses the mind, prepares the instrument for work, and helps prevent strain and tiredness. The following general exercises should be incorporated into a rehearsal routine, and if possible combined with the warm-up strategies listed under 'Warming up' for each song.

☐ Physical warm-up routines

The whole body is involved in singing. The aim of warming up is to move, flex, and stretch the body for good posture, and suppleness when singing. We want balance, coordination, freedom, and ease, so there is no strain in the body, or in the sound.

- Wake up by shaking body parts, and slapping arms, legs, and chest.
- Play some rhythmic clapping games to focus attention.
- Stretch slowly outwards and upwards with the arms, feeling tall and wide.
- Stand tall—shoulders back but not rigid, head feeling loose on top, feet slightly apart.
- Lift arms up in front, breathing in slowly; hold, then breathe out slowly.
- Breathe in slowly (say to a count of four slow beats); hold, then hiss the air out.
- Massage face and neck, particularly the jaw line and cheeks.
- Pull silly faces to mobilize the eyes and jaws; wiggle tongues.
- Chew some very sticky imaginary toffee to loosen the jaw.

☐ Vocal warm-up routines

The aim here is to start voicing sounds, warming up the vocal cords, and beginning to stretch the vocal range.

- Breathe deeply and hum long notes, increasing the intensity by getting louder.
- Yawn loudly, extending the pitch range.
- Sirening—make a 'ng' sound at the back of your throat, sustain it, and make a sirening sound up and down, as high and low as possible. This stretches the voice and settles the larynx.
- Sing some five-note scale exercises quietly to the sound 've'.
- Sing the words 'are there bees on you?' up and down the first five notes of the scale to practise the five vowel sounds.
- Sing scales rapidly up and down with short *staccato* notes to 'la', 'ma', and 'da'.
- Sing up and down arpeggios or broken chords to any syllable with consonant attached, raising the arms to 'paint' the shape of the phrases.
- Sing some simple rounds or call and response songs from the *Voiceworks* 1 and 2 collections to extend the exercises more musically.

☐ Vocal warm-up exercises

These simple exercises are useful warm-up routines, and link with some of the songs in the book (for example, the first to No. 7 'Run go a Kingston', the second to No. 8 'Jane an' Louisa'). Try them in different keys to stretch the voices. Exercise 2 can be sung as a canon starting at *.

Ex. 1

key change

noo noo noo etc.

Ex. 2

key change

noo noo noo   noo noo noo   noo__ noo noo.   noo noo noo   noo noo noo   noo__ noo noo.

◻ Four warm-up songs

At the start of a rehearsal or workshop, it's important to get people singing quickly with cheerful assurance and confidence. Within minutes of starting, your group could be singing a simple Jamaican folksong or round, or even a multi-part reggae style backing. The following songs all contain features that are typical of most of the songs in this collection—repetition in the melodies; simple harmony patterns; syncopated rhythm patterns; short riffs. The three solo songs come from the community and the words reflect their origins and traditions.

Linstead Train

Linstead is an important market town in the central highlands of Jamaica. The town is remembered in the popular song 'Linstead Market' and was once connected to the capital city, Kingston, by a railway line which carried passenger trains on a tortuous route through the dramatic Bog Walk Gorge to the south. Today the line has been re-opened for freight trains which serve the bauxite/alumina mines near Ewarton, a few miles to the north-west of Linstead.

'Linstead Train' is a simple game song which was, no doubt, originally played to help pass the time at the station as passengers awaited the arrival of their train. The participants form two lines, linking arms together. They then shuffle forwards and backwards, relative to the space which is available to them, moving in time to the crotchet beat of the song melody.

Teach the song a phrase at a time (four bars each), starting in any key that is comfortable for the lead singer. When it has been confidently learnt try sharing out the phrases between different groups of singers. Add some movement as suggested in the notes above, and change the pulse/tempo to get singers used to listening to each other and working as a team. Aim for a strong sound with a full tone.

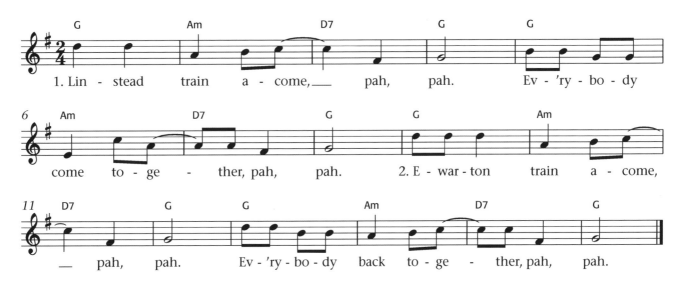

1. Lin - stead train a - come,__ pah, pah.   Ev - 'ry - bo - dy
come to - ge - ther, pah, pah.   2. E - war - ton train a - come,
__ pah, pah.   Ev - 'ry - bo - dy back to - ge - ther, pah, pah.

Horsehead

This simple dance song belongs to the Jamaican Jonkunnu tradition. This tradition dates back to slavery and is associated with Christmas festivities, when entertainments were staged involving music and dance, and featuring slaves wearing costumes and masks.

As the tradition developed so distinct Jonkunnu characters became established. The most notable of these characters are the 'Horsehead', and the 'Jack in de Green'. The former character wears a horse-mask and leans on a wooden crutch, hidden under fabric, to simulate the four-legged animal in question. And the latter wears both hat and mask to set off a costume of green leaves and foliage.

Jonkunnu dancing has its origins in the African Ashanti dance tradition and is accompanied by fife (a bamboo flute) and drums. Christmas celebrations in Jamaica sometimes feature processions through villages which are led by Jonkunnu groups.

Teach the song as a call and response, then divide the singers into two groups and get each group to take turns in leading; keep the pulse steady. This is a good introduction to the typical Jamaican syncopated rhythm (e.g. bar 5; and a tied version in bar 2), so work the song until this is firmly established with confidence.

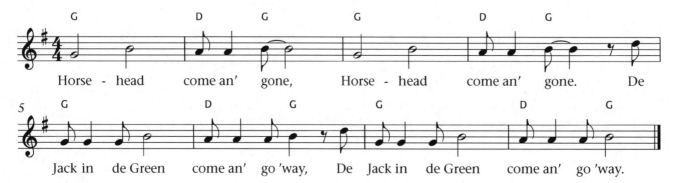

When I go home

Like No. 2 'Run, Moses, run', this song uses a melody which belongs to the quadrille tradition (see p. x). The quadrille dates from slavery and is a set of dances of European origin, played in the plantation owner's house on festive occasions. The set consists of five dances (or, properly, figures) of which the first is in triple (or compound) metre. 'When I go home' is an example of a first figure melody and should be sung with a dance-like swing which emphasizes the moderately paced dotted-crotchet beat.

The words of the song relate to the fact that British soldiers based in Jamaica when it was a colony were often attracted to Jamaican women, and vice versa. Here one soldier undertakes to tell his mother about the Jamaican girls he claims 'won't leave him alone' when he returns to Britain.

Teach the song a phrase at a time (two bars), taking care with the repeated notes in the middle of the phrases. This can be sung as a canon at two-bar intervals—a good way of building confidence and independent singing leading to parts.

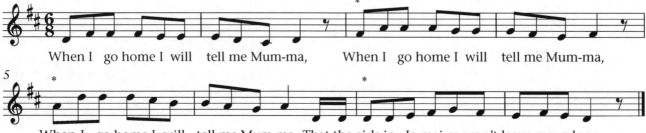

Step up, wake up

The reggae songs of Bob Marley are often characterized by a very simple harmonic structure (one or two chords), a bass riff, off-beat chords, and simple short motivic melody phrases. This warm-up piece pulls these ideas together to get a group singing in harmony. Start with the bass-line—the rhythm and pulse should be strong and very clear; then add the harmony, starting with one note and gradually building the whole chord. Finally add the melody, then the echo melody. Extra melodies and words can be added and the whole exercise treated very freely, provided the singers move together, get into a groove, and really feel what they are doing.

Repeat the sequence as many times as you like; when it's time to finish, give a signal and go on to the last time bar. Alternatively, do the reverse of the opening by fading out the parts one at a time, ending with the bass.

Dance and Humorous Songs

1 You walk an' talk

RESOURCES ▶ CD1 track 1 (performance); CD2 track 1 (backing)

You need to know

This satirical song takes a wry look at the role of the village gossip in creating confusion among the local inhabitants. Even the simplest things—borrowing cooking ingredients or glancing in the pot on the stove, walking into a room, or looking out of a door—have unforeseen consequences. And when it comes to passing on what Sue or Lou said in conversation, or discussing the activities of Jim or Jack, the village gossip always puts her foot in it.

The satirical elements and social context of 'You walk an' talk' link the song to African–Caribbean tradition and the song can be given a 'mento' feel by emphasizing the fourth beat of each bar in performance (see No. 4 'Mango Walk').

In Jamaican colloquial usage the words 'this', 'that', and 'there' would be pronounced as 'dis', 'dat', and 'dere', thus giving the song a more percussive edge. You may feel that these phoneticizations should be introduced into your performances for this reason.

Warming up

- Practise being neighbourhood gossips! In pairs or small groups have animated conversations about unimportant issues, taking turns to spread some news or complaint.
- Warm up bodies by introducing gestures and finger wagging.
- Sing the phrase 'You beg a little this' (bar 6b–7) up and down the first five notes of the scale. 'You' should be shortened more colloquially to 'yu'.
- Extend this to a whole octave before learning the harmony part.
- Make the sound *staccato* and crisp—match the gossipy/irritated voices from the first exercise.

Teaching and learning

- Sing the melody in unison, and get it really confident. It can be taught by rote as it is so simple and repetitive; the rhythm changes come easily with the natural inflection of the words.
- Sing all three verses before adding any harmony—this is essentially a unison song and needs to be strong on its own first.
- Teach the harmony part by rote to everyone. Depending on the confidence of the singers, either divide the group in half and put the two parts together quickly, or sing one part yourself while they (or a small group) sing the other to demonstrate the effect.

- Teach the short descant passage to a small group, or make it an instrumental part.

Listen out

- Are the voices chatty and conversational? Make sure they are *staccato* and not too lyrical. (The only held or sustained notes must be at the end of each section—bars 6b, 14, and 18b.)
- Are the pick-up or upbeat notes (e.g. bars 2 and 6b) together and confident? If everyone breathes well in advance there should be no problem.
- Is everybody singing with crisp rhythms and words together? Remember that 'you' should be shortened to 'yu', and 'this', 'that', and 'there' can be pronounced 'dis', 'dat', and 'dere'.
- As always with this style, stress the characteristic syncopated (or off-beat) notes and not the main beats of the bar, e.g. 'look **in** a pot' (bar 11).
- Does the harmony part stay in tune as it rises (e.g. bars 8–10)? Return to some warm-up scales if this isn't happening.

Performing

- This song needs to be robust and full of life and humour; aim to bring this out with clear words and even some solos and individual characterization.
- Solo singers can take more liberty with the rhythms and even embellish the melody as the mood takes them.
- In performance, actions or dramatic gestures could be added, or standing in 'freeze frame' tableaux to illustrate each verse.
- Suggested performance plan: unison verse 1; introduce harmony in verse 2—sing quietly to reflect more personal conversations; louder verse 3, adding the descant for a strong final chorus.

1 You walk an' talk

* Verses 2 and 3 are given on page 6.

This page may be photocopied

Verse 2

2. You say Sue say, an' you say Lou say, an' you bring con - fu - sion there. Oh! you

2. You say Sue say, say Lou say, bring con - fu - sion there. Oh! you

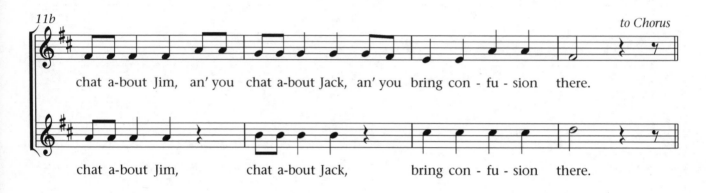

to Chorus

chat a-bout Jim, an' you chat a-bout Jack, an' you bring con - fu - sion there.

chat a-bout Jim, chat a-bout Jack, bring con - fu - sion there.

Verse 3

3. You look in a hall, an' you walk in a room, an' you bring con - fu - sion there. Oh! you

3. You look in a hall, walk in a room, bring con - fu - sion there. Oh! you

to Final Chorus

look out a door, an' you move out a yard, an' you bring con - fu - sion there.

look out a door, move out a yard, bring con - fu - sion there.

This page may be photocopied

2 Run, Moses, run

RESOURCES ▶ CD1 track 2 (performance); CD2 track 2 (backing)

You need to know

The serious theme that underlies this apparently light-hearted dance song is that of slavery. For Moses is a slave attempting to escape from the control of Mr Walker, the man employed by the slave-owner to oversee work on the plantation. The penalties for slaves trying to escape were severe, so Moses is told to run and never try to look back, even if he trips up ('buck your foot') in his haste. The melody of 'Run, Moses, run' stems from the quadrille, a set of dances of European origin played at celebratory occasions in the plantation owner's house (see p. x). The house was often well built and of a size commensurate with the owner's status. His family and friends would dance to the polkas, waltzes, and mazurkas of the quadrille, and the slaves soon learnt to play the dance tunes on their own, self-made instruments. They also imitated the dance movements of the English settlers, no doubt poking fun at the formal way in which their oppressors enjoyed themselves.

'Run, Moses, run' is derived from a mazurka, a dance of Polish origin which is played and danced with a strong accent on the first beat of each bar. The dance movements that became associated with the mazurka in Jamaica involve a long step on the first beat followed by a short step on each of the second and third beats of the bar.

Warming up

- Do some gentle stretching and deep, slow breathing exercises.
- Sing up and down some arpeggios, both *staccato* and *legato*.
- Practise the exercise below, changing key to stretch the voices.

Run, Mo-ses, run, Mo-ses, run. (breathe)

Teaching and learning

- Teach the melody to everyone, a phrase at a time, using call and response. Make sure that the notes are accurate and in tune.
- Make the notes fairly detached and full of energy, but keep the waltz-like feel.
- Teach everyone the harmony part and, by contrast, sing it smoothly but with shorter crotchet notes at the ends of phrases. Notice that bars 14*b*–22 (second half) match bars 7–14 (first half).

- When both parts are confident, divide the singers into two equal groups and put them together.

Listen out

- Are the melody notes in tune? They move mostly by leap in the first section (e.g. bars 7 and 8) so it is likely that not all the singers are landing on them accurately. If this happens, practise the phrases slowly and smoothly first—possibly to an open vowel like 'ah'—then gradually speed up and introduce the words to give some shape and energy.
- Does the harmony line sound smooth and relaxed on the long notes? Encourage this phrasing.
- In bars 15 and 19 the harmony part is pitched higher than the melody; are the singers aware of this and possibly less confident? Make sure the melody maintains its strength so it can still be heard clearly—check the balance.

Performing

- The CD recording features girls' voices only but this song can be sung by any voices, provided there is a good balance between parts.
- The sound must always be assertive but not strident, and in a steady tempo—almost a feel of one beat per bar.
- It can be performed several times through with contrasts. Suggested performance plan: melody in unison; harmony in unison; all parts together including instrument (the instrument part works well played on the flute up one octave). You could also try adding a repeat for an instrumental solo in the middle.
- The final time can either be strong, giving Moses encouragement; or get gradually quieter, as he disappears without looking back.
- When using the backing CD, sing three times, varying the scoring with each repetition.

2 Run, Moses, run

This page may be photocopied

Instrument

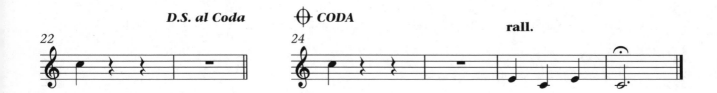

This page may be photocopied

3 Mister Potter

RESOURCES ▶ CD1 track 3 (performance); CD2 track 3 (backing)

You need to know

There is a theatrical element to this humorous song in that it sets the stage for a confrontation between two protagonists: the tenant of a house and the agent of the local landowner. The first singer to participate in the song, the tenant, is on the defensive when he greets and then confronts Mr Potter, the agent, knowing that he has not paid his rent. He complains that his attempts to grow red peas (actually beans) and yellow yam (a type of large root vegetable) on land belonging to 'red Sally' have failed due to the fact that the vegetables were eaten by the pigeons. The suggestion here is that it is as a result of the crop failures that the tenant has no money with which to pay off the rent. However, Mr Potter tells the tenant, in song, to leave his 'yard' (the ground surrounding a house, which is often fenced off) since the house rent money remains unpaid.

Like No. 5 'Fan me soldier man', 'Mister Potter' is a song with a long history within Jamaican traditional culture: both songs are quoted in Walter Jekyll's *Jamaican Song and Story*, an important collection of traditional material published in 1907.

Warming up

• Get your group to walk around the room greeting each other in any way they like.
• Chant 'mornin' to you' (harmony-part rhythm, bars 4–5) and continue to greet each other with a hand shake. Chant it with a smile—happy to greet; and with a frown—indignant and displeased!
• Sing Ex. 1 at the foot of the page. Stand still at first, then move about while singing, greeting others as you go. Try it as a canon, the second entry starting at *.

Teaching and learning

• Teach the first half of the melody (bars 2–10). Make it strong—this is a cheeky tenant coming to complain. Make the sound very conversational: clear words with no hint of sustaining any notes.
• Teach the second half (bars 10–16). Again make it good and strong, but more indignant—this is the landlord who is still owed rent!
• Divide the group in two and sing each half of the melody to each other with suitable characterization.

Swap over and change the groupings; as confidence grows get everyone to sing the whole melody together. For fun, and confidence building when learning, the melody works as a canon, starting at * and using the canon accompaniment. Note the slight word change for verse 2: 'yellow yam' instead of 'red peas'.
• Teach the harmony in stages. Start with 'mornin' to you' (bars 4–5 and 6–7) as chanted in the warm up. Extend this by singing 'come out me yard now sir' (bars 11–12), which is the same plus two notes on the end; a small group can add these riffs in the appropriate places. The remaining harmony phrases can be learnt by rote, starting with the cadence in bars 14–16.
• Add the descant once these parts sound confident; it could be played on an instrument. This part can be a little more *legato*, almost sounding like the bystanders watching this extraordinary exchange.

Listen out

• Are the upbeat notes confident, and are all the singers together? Make sure they breathe in good time and are aware that the first note and word are very important.
• Compare the melody in bars 10–11 and 12–13 ('come out a me yard'); has everyone spotted the difference? Make sure the quaver upbeats are accurate.
• Is everyone singing in the same light and jaunty way with clear words? Encourage a bright and open face to give the right tone, and avoid sustained singing.
• How is the rhythm sounding? Singers should enjoy the characteristic syncopated pattern (e.g. harmony part, bar 4), and must take care not to rush any repeated quavers (e.g. bar 7).
• When all voices are together there is quite a lot going on—like the conversations—so make sure the final phrase is clearly together and very declamatory.

Performing

• The addition of a bass instrument doubling the piano left hand will add some character.
• Suggested performance plan: unison melody (perhaps divided into two groups as above); repeat and add harmony (words from either verse); all three parts together—possibly with instrument on the descant, if singers only want to divide into two parts.
• When using the backing CD, sing three times.

Ex. 1

Good morn - in' Mis - ter Pot - ter an' good morn - in' to you sir! (Good)

3 Mister Potter

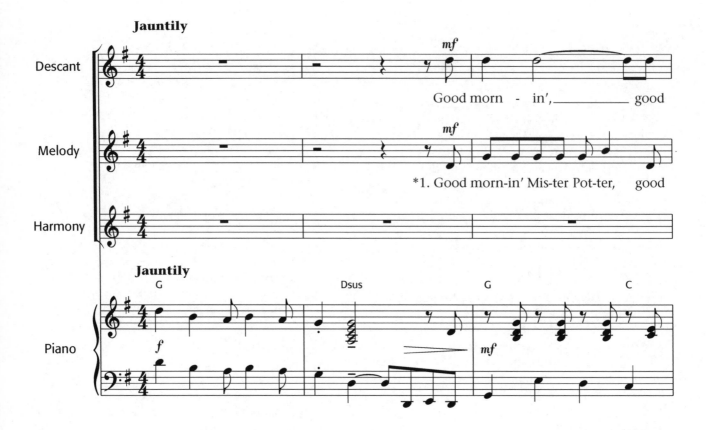

* Verse 2 has the same words as verse 1, except that 'red peas' is replaced by 'yellow yam' in bars 7 and 8.

This page may be photocopied

© Oxford University Press 2009

This page may be photocopied

Canon accompaniment

This page may be photocopied

4 Mango Walk

RESOURCES ► CD1 track 4 (performance); CD2 track 4 (backing)

☐ You need to know

This is one of the best known of Jamaican traditional melodies. Indeed, it was first popularized in the UK during the 1930s when Arthur Benjamin used it as the basis of a composition in which he identified the tune as a 'rumba'. In fact, the rumba is a Cuban dance form and 'Mango Walk' belongs to the Jamaican national dance song tradition called 'mento' (the equivalent in Caribbean terms of merengue from the Dominican Republic and calypso from Trinidad and Tobago).

Mento songs are performed at a steady pace and their melodies provide the framework for singers to comment, in witty and often satirical fashion, on people and events in their local communities. In musical terms, the rhythms of mento are less complex than those of rumba or calypso and short rhythmic units are used repetitively, as with the syncopated ♪ ♩ ♪ figure found here. A characteristic of mento style is emphasizing the final crotchet beat of each 4/4 bar.

In this version of 'Mango Walk' the singer is requesting assurance from the person listening (the 'darling' referred to in the chorus) that they did not steal ('pick up') a mango of the size and type known as a 'number 'leven'. A phoneticization used is 'fe' (in order to).

A recording of 'Mango Walk' by the mento band The Happy Smilers is included on CD2 (track 23). This gives an idea of how the song sounds using traditional instruments and vocal styles.

☐ Warming up

- Begin by singing the harmony 2 part for bars 5–8; this simple riff will establish the syncopated rhythm and the two chords that make up the backing.
- Walk around the room and invent a 'mango walk'—emphasize the syncopation with lots of hip movement!
- Add the harmony 1 part for colour and variety.

☐ Teaching and learning

- Teach the first half of the melody (bars 4–12). This tune is reasonably well known so take extra care to be accurate, especially when there are large leaps between notes (e.g. bars 6 and 7). Sing it slowly to check if necessary.
- The words should be crisp and clear— more *staccato* singing than *legato*—really emphasizing the first syllable of '**man**go'. Try to pronounce 'that' as 'dat', and 'the' as 'de'.

- Teach the second half (bars 13–20), picking out the similarities with the first half when there are large leaps. Notice that 'true' in bar 15 is on a different note from 'Walk' in bar 7, even though the rest of the pattern is the same.
- Return to the backing riffs (harmony 1 and 2) and revise them. Then work on the second half, making sure that bars 13–14 and 17–18 are smoother, giving the minims their full length, but without overpowering the melody.
- Put all three parts together, with a few more singers on the melody to create the right balance. Finally add the instrument. Do you recognize the melody? It is connected with two more fruits!

☐ Listen out

- Is the sound spirited, without feeling rushed and too energetic? Make sure the quavers in bars 5 and 9 don't run away.
- Is everyone singing the large leaps accurately? If not, do more slow singing so that everyone can really hear the notes and get to grips with them.
- What is the balance like in bars 13–14 and 17–19? Ensure the higher harmony 1 notes don't dominate the sound.
- Make sure the last two bars are emphatic but not too aggressive.

☐ Performing

- This song can be sung by any combination of voices. If changed voices are involved, it's best to keep them on the melody or split them between the melody and one harmony part; avoid putting them all on the harmony parts as the texture could sound too 'thick' or heavy.
- Keep the sound witty and light throughout, and make the second half a little more pleading (see 'You need to know', above).
- Suggested performance plan: verse 1 ('mumma')— unison melody; verse 2 ('brother')—add both harmony parts; verse 3 ('sister')—all parts and instrument. For a longer performance try adding the harmony parts one at a time, repeating verse 1 at the end.
- This arrangement works well *a cappella*; perhaps one verse could feature this.
- The backing track presents a fuller accompaniment for this song to liven up performances. When using the backing CD, sing through three times.

4 Mango Walk

* Other verses: replace 'mumma' each time with 'brother' for verse 2 and 'sister' for verse 3.

This page may be photocopied

Instrument

Steady

last time **to Coda** ⊕

⊕ *CODA*

This page may be photocopied

5 Fan me soldier man

RESOURCES ▶ CD1 track 5 (performance); CD2 track 5 (backing 1), track 6 (backing 2)

You need to know

This popular dance tune is one of a number of traditional songs which refer to soldiers and the military. In Jamaica, being a soldier is a sought-after profession and, even under colonization, young women often saw the occupying English soldiers as romantic figures. In 'Fan me soldier man' the woman is being partnered by a soldier at a local dance. The terms 'wheel', 'turn', and 'swing' describe specific dance actions and, as with many Jamaican traditional tunes, it is important to set a moderate tempo in performance, so as to enable the dancers to manage the actions without being rushed. Such a tempo also allows the musicians in the dance band to play accompaniments which, characteristically, are quite busy rhythmically.

'Fan me soldier man' has its origins as one of a set of dances known as a quadrille (see p. x). As a genre the quadrille dates back to slavery when European dances such as the waltz and polka were brought to Jamaica by the plantation owners. Such forms are featured in the quadrille, which comprises five figures, or dances. The melody of 'Fan me soldier man' is an example of a quadrille fifth figure. As such, its objective was to bring the quadrille set to a lively conclusion. The song's long history is demonstrated by the fact that it is notated in Walter Jekyll's *Jamaican Song and Story*, published in 1907.

A recording of 'Fan me soldier man' by the mento band The Happy Smilers is included on CD2 (track 24). This gives an idea of how this song sounds using traditional instruments and vocal styles.

Warming up

- Practise good standing positions—feet slightly apart, standing tall, relaxed shoulders.
- Do some slow breathing exercises: in and out for a count of four, then six, then eight.
- Sing the exercise below, starting in any key. Concentrate on acquiring a smooth sound, but with quiet energy and excitement in the rhythm and words. Try it as a canon starting at *.

Fan me sol-dier man, fan me sol-dier man,

key change

fan me sol-dier man, fan me.

Teaching and learning

- Everyone should learn the melody first, making sure the word 'soldier' is given due emphasis. The word 'with' should sound more like 'wid'.
- Keep the tempo steady but give some energy to the rhythms through the words.
- Add the harmony next as it shadows the tune and echoes it in bars 6 and 8; make sure the last note (unison G) is in tune.
- Teach the descant last, making sure that the phrases in bars 6 and 8 are accurate (the notes in bar 8 are the same as bar 6 backwards). To get the rhythm accurate, speak the first bar of the melody ('Fan me soldier man') and clap instead of saying 'Fan'. Do this repeatedly until it sounds confident.
- Sing all three parts together, making sure that the melody can be heard and that the descant does not dominate. Really enjoy bars 10–12 where the parts come together; make this strong.

Listen out

- Does the song sound convincing? Do the singers sound as though they want the attention of the soldiers?! Decide if they are yearning for attention in their imaginations, or being bold and outspoken—this will make a difference to the vocal sound and volume.
- Is the word 'soldier' emphasized enough? Accent it slightly, and make the 'l' really strong.
- What is the balance like? Check that the descant is not too loud.

Performing

- The words suggest a female-only performance, but the choice is yours!
- The descant could be played by an instrument.
- There is scope for a lot of variation, repeating as often as you like. CD performance plan: verse 1 ('Fan me')—melody only; verse 2 ('Hold me')—melody and descant; verse 3 ('Swing me')—all three parts. An alternative would be to add the harmony first, before adding the descant, as the melody and harmony parts make a nice duet.
- You could add the percussion lines one at a time for each verse; try using them for the introduction too.
- Two backings are provided for this song: backing 1 includes the notated percussion parts, while backing 2 is piano only, to give groups the option to add these themselves.

5 Fan me soldier man

Easily

* Other verses: replace 'fan' each time with 'hold' for verse 2 and 'swing' for verse 3.

This page may be photocopied

fan me, fan me, oh, come wheel an' turn with me.

fan me sol - dier man, fan me, oh, come wheel an' turn with me.

fan me sol - dier man, fan me, oh, come wheel an' turn with me.

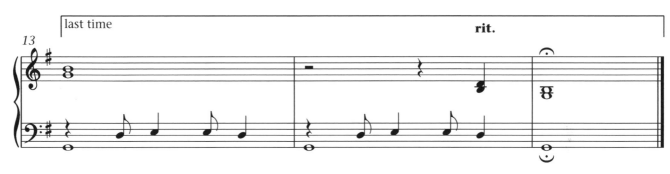

last time   **rit.**

Suggested percussion patterns

repeat as necessary

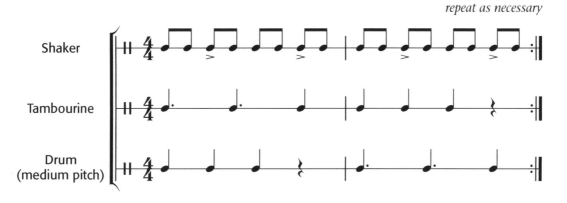

Shaker

Tambourine

Drum (medium pitch)

This page may be photocopied

6 Jackass with the long tail

RESOURCES ▶ CD1 track 6 (performance); CD2 track 7 (backing)

You need to know

The jackass, or donkey, was commonly used as a beast of burden in Jamaica and is still used as such in some areas today. The animal provides the means of carrying vegetables, fruit, and coffee between farming plots, settlements, and markets. Indeed, in the mountainous districts of Jamaica the jackass comes into its own because it is adept at managing the often steep and narrow paths which wind their way through the lush landscape there. This particular jackass has a long tail, apparently; perhaps the tail can be grasped by its owner to help keep the animal steady as it makes its way down a particularly precipitous slope.

The goods to be carried by the jackass are loaded into large baskets or panniers ('hampas') strapped to its back. It is obviously important that these containers are packed in such a way as to distribute the load equally if the animal is to keep a firm footing. And, clearly, teasing or squeezing the jackass while it is in motion will distract it from the task in hand.

The 'coco' referred to in the song is not cocoa but cocohead, a root vegetable which, in Jamaica, constitutes a staple starch food. Jamaica's Blue Mountain coffee is widely recognized as the finest in the world, the island's climate and high tropical rain forest providing the ideal setting for the farming of the crop.

Warming up

- After some physical stretching and general vocal warm ups, sing the exercise below in different keys; start in E♭ and work up to G major.

- Find a steady pulse to match the crotchet beat, and walk it on the spot.
- Speak or chant the words of bars 3–6, maintaining the walking pulse. Take care as the rhythm is different in each bar. Make sure 'bag of coco' in bar 5 is snappy, after the silent first beat. Note that bars 11–14 are exactly the same as bars 3–6.

Teaching and learning

- Begin with the melody, keeping the rhythm and sense of pulse from the warm up.
- Work on the middle section (bars 6b–10); here the rhythm is more consistent. Make sure the crotchets in bar 9 are laid back and don't rush. The singers should stop the sound with each comma (after 'him'), and the sound should be stronger and more commanding than that of the first section.
- Sing all three verses—you could even make up extra verses using other crops.
- Add the bass part next. Keep it gentle, and make sure the syncopated rhythm is accurate and supports the melody, particularly in bar 5 where the emphasis is slightly different. In bar 6a ('comin' down') and bar 10 ('squeezie him'), don't take a breath before the next bar; slur the sound across the bar line to keep the momentum.
- Add harmony 2 next. It only has three notes, and matches the bass part in bars 6b–10.
- Finally add harmony 1. This partners harmony 2 in the first section, but in the middle section it partners the melody, so make it a bit stronger here.

Listen out

- Is the balance right in the outer two sections? Make sure the harmony doesn't dominate.
- What is the ensemble like in the middle section? The voices should be rhythmic and together; be careful not to rush in bar 9.

Performing

- The harmony and bass parts are simple and could also be played on instruments, such as bass guitar or cello for the bass part and clarinet or viola for the harmony. This would add a new dimension to the song.
- Suggested performance plan: verse 1—melody only (upper voices); verse 2—melody and bass part; verse 3—all parts and instrument. (The instrument part works well played an octave higher on the flute.) Another possibility would be to introduce the harmony parts, one at a time or together, before adding the bass.
- For a longer performance, sing verse 1 again or make up a new verse.
- When using the backing CD, sing through three times.

6 Jackass with the long tail

* Other verses: replace 'coco' each time with 'mango' for verse 2 and 'coffee' for verse 3.

This page may be photocopied

tea-sie him, No make him ham-pa squee-zie him. Jack-ass_ with the

tea-sie him, No make him ham-pa squee-zie him. ah _____

tea-sie him, No make him ham-pa squee-zie, squee-zie him. do do__

long tail, Bag of *co - co* com-in' down. No com-in' down.

(*ah*) _____ No __

do do__ do do__ do No do

Instrument

Gentle and relaxed

This page may be photocopied

7 Run go a Kingston

RESOURCES ▶ CD1 track 7 (performance); CD2 track 8 (backing)

You need to know

Kingston is the capital city of Jamaica and one of the country's main shopping centres. The city is built on a plain which rises gently to the lower slopes of the Blue Mountains, whose peaks dominate the skyline to the north. For people living in the mountains and surrounding country districts, Kingston is the place to which they come to sell their goods and make their purchases.

In this song, the performer fantasizes about sending someone into the city to buy a 'lahma gown' for her. 'Lahma' is the Jamaican colloquial version of the word 'lamé', meaning a garment fashioned from a fabric decorated with gold or silver thread (see also No. 13 'Christmas a come'). The likelihood is, of course, that such a gown would be too expensive for the ordinary country dweller to buy. Indeed, this point is reinforced by the singer's reference to the fantasy that it would be 'worth a thousand pound'.

Other Jamaican expressions used are 'a' (to) and 'fe' (in order to).

Warming up

- Start with some slow deep breathing—in and out to a slow count.
- Sing Exercise 1 on p. xiii to 'noo', then to different vowel sounds ('ni', 'ne', 'na'), raising the pitch each time.
- Encourage singers to do the whole exercise all in one breath; control the airflow.

Teaching and learning

- Start with the melody in bars 5–12: make it smooth as in the exercise, but with a breath in bar 8. Try making 'thousand' sound more like 'tousan''; and 'pound' sound like 'poun''.
- The pace should be steady, but with an excited feeling of anticipation.
- Learn the bass-line next—the rhythm is the same as that of the melody—then put them together.
- Tackle the same two voice parts for the middle section (bars 13–20). Don't make the 'Glory allelu' sound too pure; keep an open sound so that it sounds like 'glahry', and more colloquial.
- Bars 21–9 are the same as the first section (with a longer final note), so now you can put the whole piece together.

- For the harmony part, look at the middle section first (bars 14–20). The start of each phrase picks up from the melody, and then finishes with a descending scale before the cadence.
- Put the melody and harmony in this middle section together first, and then add the bass part. Make the dynamics effective: gradually build up, and remember to drop back down to *mp* on the repeat.
- Finally learn the harmony part for the first section. It is a kind of echo of the melody. Check that the interval jumps in bars 7–8 are accurate.
- The final section should be strong, but notice the long held note with a diminuendo at the end.

Listen out

- What do the words sound like? Don't make them too strong, but keep them clear enough to be understood.
- Is the melody in tune in bars 6 and 7? The repeated notes at either end of each bar can go flat, so make sure that the last note is well supported with enough breath.
- What is the balance like? The three voices can be almost equal in volume, particularly in the middle section where the parts imitate each other, but the harmony part mustn't overdo it in bar 17 where the melody is low.

Performing

- This simple folksong works well with a good strong rendering of the melody; begin like that, with all voices in unison, and then add other parts.
- CD performance plan: bars 1–20—melody only with repeats; back to the beginning with all parts and sing through to the end. Follow this structure when using the backing track.
- The bass and harmony parts could be added one at a time, so that the whole song is performed three times.
- Add some variety by changing the dynamics; try singing very quietly for the repeats, or for the whole of the second time through.

7 Run go a Kingston

This page may be photocopied

pound. Glo - ry al - le - lu, glo - ry al - le - lu,

gown. Glo - ry al - le - lu, glo - ry al - le -

pound. Glo - ry al - le - lu, glo - ry al - le - lu,

glo - ry al - le - lu, it worth a thou - sand pound. pound.

-lu,___ al - le - lu,___ it worth a thou - sand pound. pound.

glo - ry al - le - lu, it worth a thou - sand pound. pound.

This page may be photocopied

Run go a King-ston fe buy me lah - ma gown. When me lah - ma

Run go a King-ston, run go a

Run go a King-ston fe buy me lah - ma gown. When me lah - ma

D   F#m   G   D   G

dress come it worth a thou-sand pound._____

King-ston fe buy me lah - ma gown._____

dress come it worth a thou-sand pound._____

D   Em   A   D   G   D

rall.   Slower

This page may be photocopied

Section II

Work and Ring-Game Songs

8 Jane an' Louisa

RESOURCES ▶ CD1 track 8 (performance); CD2 track 9 (backing)

☐ You need to know

Children's ring-games have always played an important role in Jamaican culture, the lasting popularity of many of the melodies associated with the games being one indicator of this importance. Some song lyrics and melodies are derived from English ring-games, having been transmitted by missionaries who set up schools in Jamaica during the 19th century. Others, such as 'Jane an' Louisa', have their origins in the Edwardian music hall and were taken to the island by English sailors and settlers. Subsequently, of course, the songs have become thoroughly Jamaican in theme, language, and movement. The game played to 'Jane an' Louisa' consists of the following activities:

(a) The participants form a ring leaving two girls, Jane and Louisa, outside the ring and some distance away from it;
(b) As the children sing verse 1 the two girls walk slowly towards the circle, typically taking a step on the first beat of each bar;
(c) During verse 2 the girls move in opposite directions around, and in close proximity to, the ring of children. As they go round they pretend to pluck a rose from each participant;
(d) Jane and Louisa then each select a partner from the ring and, as the children sing verse 3, they and their partners enter the ring and dance within it, basing their movements loosely on those of the waltz.

A recording of 'Jane an' Louisa' by the mento band The Happy Smilers is included on CD2 (track 25). This gives an idea of how this song sounds using traditional instruments and vocal styles.

☐ Warming up

- Begin with some scale exercises to warm up the voices.
- Sing Exercise 2 on p. xiii to different vowel sounds, with a soft consonant at the start—aim for a smooth and flowing dancing sound. Try it as a canon, the second entry starting at *.
- Now sing it while swinging arms from side to side and swaying as if dancing.

☐ Teaching and learning

- Everyone should enjoy singing the melody first, with a slow one-in-a–bar lilt to it. Imagine the Edwardian music hall atmosphere, and give it some character. Support the rising notes in bars 15–16.

- Take care with the pronunciation: relax the sound so that 'this beautiful garden' becomes 'dis beau**d**iful garden' and 'with' becomes 'wid'—but don't be too obvious about it. Also relax the word 'to' to become 'tu' with a shortened vowel.
- Teach the harmony part to everyone: it is so simple and can give all the singers the experience of a lower part. The 'ah' should flow without a break between notes.
- Sing bars 17–18 slowly to make sure the tuning is accurate on 'beau-' in bar 18.
- Divide the singers into two equal groups and put the parts together for verse 2; swap them over for verse 3.

☐ Listen out

- Is everyone reaching the top E in bar 16 confidently and with a full tone? Make sure the singers breathe well enough to support it; the crescendo will help, as will swaying the arms and lifting them above the head on the top note. Check the rising notes in bars 18–19 in the same way.
- Are the words clear but relaxed? If necessary, speak the words to check everyone understands the effect that is required.
- Do the parts balance? Either ask those on the melody to sing more loudly, or have fewer voices on the harmony part.

☐ Performing

- The CD performance features girls' voices only, but it does not have to be done this way. In the ring-game, Jane and Louisa enter the circle and choose a partner each, which could be boys or men with changed voices.
- If the song is performed as a ring-game, it could be sung through many times with different pairs starting each time; a 'concert performance' could end with a final unison rendition of the melody.
- Suggested performance plan: verse 1—melody; verse 2—melody plus 'ah's in the harmony part, to vary the texture; verse 3—melody plus complete harmony part.

8 Jane an' Louisa

This page may be photocopied

This page may be photocopied

9 Breadfruit an' jerk pork

RESOURCES ▶ CD1 track 9 (performance); CD2 track 10 (backing)

☐ You need to know

It was common, during slavery and subsequently, for gangs of labourers to sing as they worked, responding to the musical initiative of one member of the group and matching their movements to the beat of the song. 'Breadfruit an' jerk pork' is an example of such a work song.

The song mentions two popular Jamaican dishes, anticipating their consumption by the labourers at the end of their work shift: breadfruit and jerk pork, which is particularly associated with the north coast parish of Portland, and, in verse 2, ackee and saltfish, the island's national dish. The first of these dishes is made by cutting the grapefruit-sized breadfruit into segments and then boiling or roasting it. The spicy jerk seasoning used to flavour the pork is made from allspice, scotch bonnet peppers, and cumin. In the second case, the flesh of the ackee is scraped from the fruit and fried, soon taking on the consistency of scrambled eggs. Boiled saltfish (usually cod, and salted as a preservative) is then added to the ackee, together with onions and hot peppers.

The original call and response structure of 'Breadfruit an' jerk pork' can be emphasized in performance by a) omitting the harmony and bass parts from the call phrases and b) ensuring that the response sections ('just give me here') are each sung more loudly than the preceding call phrase.

☐ Warming up

- Chant the following phrase: 'Breadfruit an' jerk **pork**—two, three, four', with a good accent on 'pork'.
- Do the same with 'Ackee an' salt**fish**—six, seven, eight'. Run the two as a continuous line.
- Repeat but leave out the numbers and insert 'just give me here' ('give me' pronounced 'gimme'); divide into two groups and share this out, call and response style. Make sure it has plenty of energy.

☐ Teaching and learning

- Teach the melody part response, 'just give me here', to everyone. Sing the calls 'Breadfruit an' jerk pork', 'Put it down . . .', and 'Keep it warm . . .' and let the group answer.
- Repeat this with verse 2, inviting other singers to join you with the calls.

- Divide the singers into two groups and sing the whole melody part call and response style. Check that the C♯ in bar 3 (on 'jerk') is really sharp and close to the Ds surrounding it—it is really just a slight 'bending' of the main note.
- Teach the bass-line next by rote; the response 'just give me here' is the same each time.
- Sing the two parts together, dividing the call and the response between groups, or getting everyone to sing all the time.
- Finally add the harmony part, ensuring that the A♯ in bar 3 (on 'jerk') is close to the surrounding Bs (as with the melody).
- Put all the parts together and check that the short notes at the end of each call (e.g. 'pork' in bar 3) are really short and crisp.

☐ Listen out

- Is the ensemble good? Make sure the rhythms are together first, and then check the tuning.
- Do everyone's words match? Check they are singing 'an" rather than 'and', and make sure all the words are shorter and less formal than pure English (e.g. 'the' and 'my' should come out as 'de' and 'ma').

☐ Performing

- On the CD this is performed by men's voices only as it is a work song, but it can be performed by any combination. It is also sung unaccompanied, which is more natural and reflects how it would have been performed originally. If done like this it can be sung in any comfortable key—just follow the leader!
- Suggested performance plan: leader sings verse 1 call, with response in unison; leader sings verse 2 call, with response including harmony and bass; all three parts sing throughout, using verse 1 words again.
- When using the backing CD, sing three times, repeating either verse.

9 Breadfruit an' jerk pork

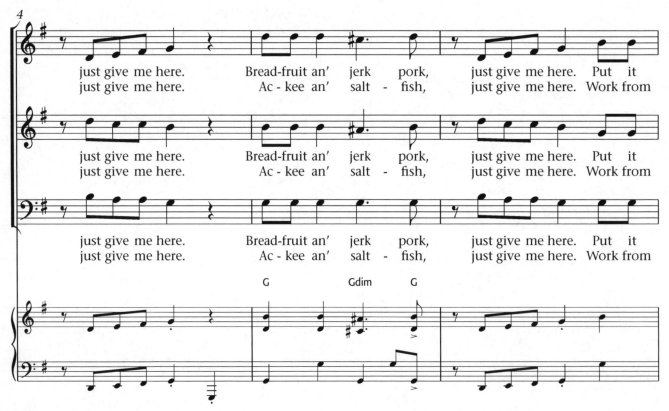

This page may be photocopied

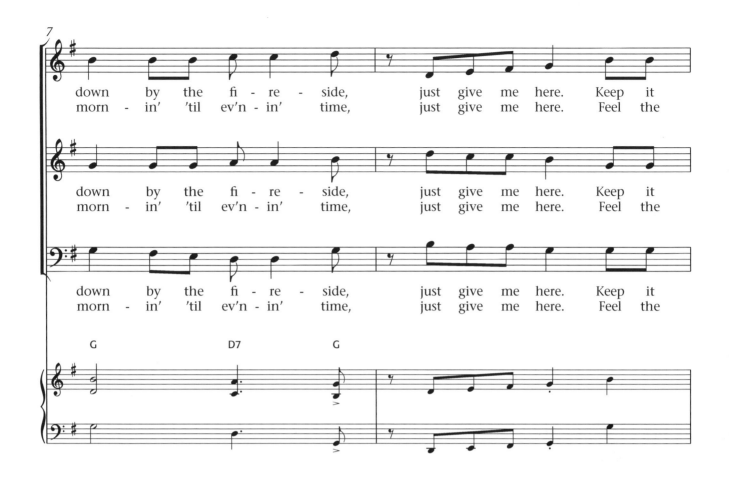

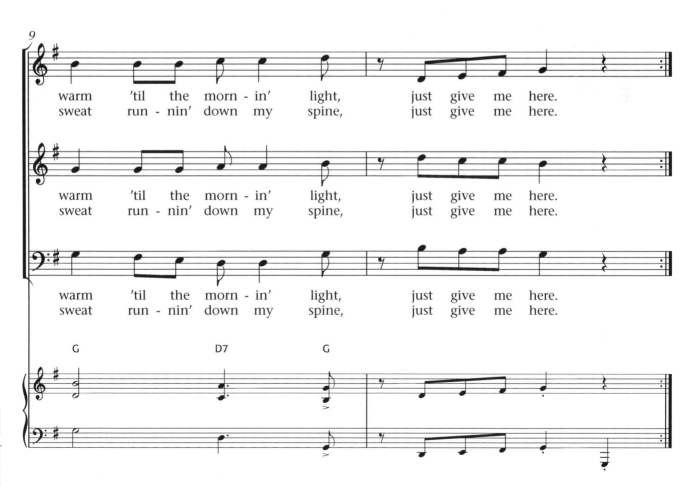

This page may be photocopied

10 Brown Girl in the Ring

RESOURCES ▶ CD1 track 10 (performance); CD2 track 11 (backing)

☐ You need to know

This ring-game song is probably the best known of all Jamaican melodies, its popularity having been reinforced by the version of the song released in 1978 by the pop group Boney M. Two of the five members of the band are from Jamaica so it was perhaps not surprising that Boney M's recording of 'Brown Girl in the Ring' was on a single containing another well-known Jamaican song, 'Rivers of Babylon' (No. 20). Almost two million copies of the single were subsequently sold in the UK and Boney M's version of 'Brown Girl in the Ring' is still often heard today. The game played to 'Brown Girl in the Ring' consists of the following activities:

(a) The participants form a ring with one child (a girl initially) standing at the centre of it. The children sing verse 1 of the song;

(b) While the participants sing verse 2, the girl in the ring skips around, in a lively fashion, within it;

(c) At the beginning of verse 3, the girl chooses and demonstrates a movement or short series of movements (termed a 'motion' in the words of the song), which the rest of the participants imitate;

(d) The girl then selects the child whom she believes to have been best at imitating her (who can be a boy, hence verse 4 of this arrangement), and that child enters the ring;

(e) The game then begins again.

A recording of 'Brown Girl in the Ring' by the mento band The Happy Smilers is included on CD2 (track 26). This gives an idea of how this song sounds using traditional instruments and vocal styles.

☐ Warming up

- Get the singers to stand in a circle and wiggle their tongues vigorously, poking them out!
- Establish a pulse (about 116 b.p.m.) and sing Ex. 1 on the following page, really using the tongues to produce a bright 'la' sound (not 'laah').
- Hold hands, sing again, and try stepping in time to the pulse as a group, taking small sidesteps as you start singing. Begin with the left foot, then close the right, and so on, where the **X** marks are in the exercise. Repeat, going to the right.
- The really adventurous can try the exercise in canon, with the second entry beginning at *. Split the group into two circles—one inside the other—and sing it while moving.

☐ Teaching and learning

- Everyone should sing the melody for verse 1 and enjoy the quirky piano accompaniment. Keep the quavers 'straight', not swung. 'There' should be softened to 'dere' for a more colloquial sound.
- Try the bass part for bars 13–22 with everyone. Treat the words as scat syllables rather than with any meaning; make the notes *staccato*, emphasizing the consonants to add a percussive quality to the sound.
- Divide the singers into two equal groups and sing the melody and bass parts for bars 13–22.
- Divide the upper voices in half so that there are three groups. The changed voices share the tune with upper voices in bars 32–40; ask one upper-voice group to sing these bars with the basses. Add the last three bars of the song at this stage if you wish.
- Sing this again, adding the second upper-voice group on the backing (top part), from bar 31. Check the individual harmony-notes for accuracy in bars 42–3.
- Next tackle the middle section (bars 22–30). Start with the melody part and then add the bass: the contrast of upper and changed voices will make it easy to hear what each part is singing. Sing it slowly, and check the join in bars 24 and 26 (from 'la' to 'then'), particularly in the bass-line.
- Now add the harmony part. Check the intervals on the words 'then you skip' and 'ocean'; notice that the notes are different the second time (bars 24–6).
- Finally invite the harmony group to look at bars 15–22. Notice that the harmony part in bars 21–2 is the same as the bass part in bars 29–30; try getting them to sing this together to check pitches.
- Sing the whole song, noting that the backing parts in bars 13–22 are alternated between the verses. Also take note of the changing dynamics in the middle section—those in brackets are for verse 3.

☐ Listen out

- Are the 'la-la-la's of the right quality, and is everyone doing the same? Ask individuals or small groups to demonstrate, and get everyone to listen.
- How is the ensemble and chording in bars 22–8? Check the tuning, and that all voices move together; sing it slowly if necessary.
- Do all singers agree on the final note of bar 30? Check it's in tune, particularly the bass part.
- Is there enough dynamic contrast? Experiment with this to achieve what works best for the singers, and agree on the size of the crescendo in bar 28.

Performing

- The piano part is important in this arrangement; make the right-hand chords very *staccato*, and the off-beat left-hand notes very rhythmic.
- Add interest to your performance by playing the ring-game (see 'You need to know', above).
- The backing CD presents a fuller accompaniment for this song to liven up performances.

Ex. 1

Tra - la - la - la - la - la,   tra - la - la - la - la - la   *etc.*

10 Brown Girl in the Ring

Jamaican trad.
arr. Kevin Stannard

With gentle energy

1. There's a brown girl in the ring, tra-la-la-la-la, There's a brown girl in the ring, tra-la-la-la-la, There's a brown girl in the ring, tra-la-la-la-la. For she like su-gar an' I like plum.

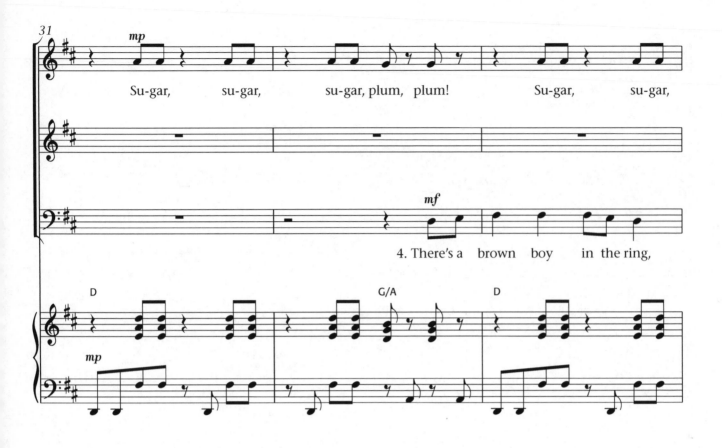

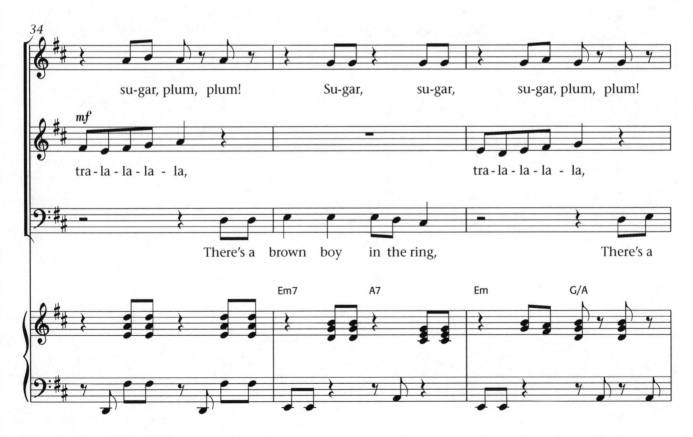

Su-gar,   su-gar,   su-gar, plum, plum!   Su-gar,   su-gar,

tra - la - la - la - la,   For   he   like   su-gar   an'

brown   boy   in the ring,   For   he   like   su-gar   an'

plum, plum, plum. For he like su-gar an' I   like   plum!

I   like plum. For he like su-gar an' I   like   plum!

I   like plum. For he like su-gar an' I   like   plum!

10 Brown Girl in the Ring

Vocal score

Jamaican trad.
arr. Kevin Stannard

With gentle energy

This page may be photocopied

This page may be photocopied

This page may be photocopied

11 Day da light

RESOURCES ▶ CD1 track 11 (performance); CD2 track 12 (backing)

☐ You need to know

The banana trade made such a significant contribution to Jamaica's economy during much of the 20th century that the fruit came to be described as the island's 'green gold'. In addition, the banana wharves such as those at Port Antonio on the north coast began to contribute to the tourist trade as the banana boats became larger and started to carry passengers who disembarked there.

'Day da light' (which means 'day is breaking') is one of the most famous of the work songs associated with the banana trade, partly as a result of Harry Belafonte's recording of it as 'The Banana Boat Song', which appeared on his *Calypso* album in 1956. The loading of bananas was often undertaken at night, partly to take advantage of the cooler temperature and partly to enable the ship to set sail at first light. It was an intensive and physically demanding job, and pacing the actions involved by linking them to the slow, steady beat of a work song could be helpful in terms of coordinating the movements of a group of labourers. In 'Day da light', the call and response patterning of the work song (see p. x) is mirrored in the use of unison voices for the call, and of voices in harmony for the response. The references to bunches of bananas consisting of up to eight 'hands' of the fruit give some idea of the weight which could be involved in lifting and carrying quantities of it.

☐ Warming up

- Sing some scales to 'veh' and 'vah' with a full tone, to stretch the voices at least an octave.
- Gently walk the pulse on the spot, then sing bars 3–4 over and over as an ostinato to get all voice parts working together from the start.
- Teach the melody by rote to everyone. Singers can keep repeating this while some of the changed voices break away to add the upper bass part.
- Next add a few singers to the lower bass part, then to the harmony, until the whole group is singing the phrase in a relaxed and confident way.

☐ Teaching and learning

- Sing bars 1–2 (the 'call') and get the singers to answer with bars 3–4 (the 'response'), as learnt in the warm up. Continue with verses 1–4 in the same way; each time the response is the same.
- Various soloists—or small groups, depending on the singers' confidence—could take turns with the calls.
- Verse 5 breaks the pattern and is essentially unison with

some imitation between the voices. Practise this slowly with all three parts together, and check the tuning up to the top E in bar 20. Note that the harmony and bass parts for the response (bars 21–2) are slightly different; look at each part separately.

- In verse 5, ensure that the notes on 'hand' (pronounced 'han') are sustained for their full length, and with a crescendo to achieve the build up towards bar 20.
- Put the whole song together, inviting different soloists (upper or changed voice) to take verses. The opening phrase should be sung by everyone and sound confident and relieved—daylight has come!

☐ Listen out

- Is the opening really confident and are the singers hitting the chord in bar 3 with accuracy? Help if necessary by singing slowly and out of tempo from 'day o' (bar 2) to 'Day' (bar 3), holding the last chord.
- Is the crescendo in bars 17–20 effective? Starting quietly will make growing in volume easier.
- How are the solos sounding? Soloists can achieve a more authentic and natural sound by adapting the calls to suit themselves—listen to our recording for inspiration!

☐ Performing

- This song needs to be sung boldly by everyone from the start, rather than building up the parts gradually like some of the other songs. However, verse 1 could be unison melody first, just for some contrast.
- An effective ending is to repeat the last four bars several times, fading out, with the piano also dropping out for the final repeat.
- The backing track presents a fuller accompaniment for this song to liven up performances. When using the backing CD, sing the last four bars three times, slowing down for the final bar.

11 Day da light

This page may be photocopied

6

tal-ly me ba-na - na. Day   da light an' me wan' go home. 2. Me come here   to-day, me may
(3.) come here   fe work, me no

Day   da light an'   me wan' go home.

Day   da light an'   me wan' go home.

A   B A/B   E   F#m B E   E

10

not come   to-mor - row. Day   da light   an'   me wan'   go home.   3. Me
come here   fe i - dle. Day   da light   an'   me wan'   go home.   4. No

Day   da light   an'   me wan'   go home.

Day   da light   an'   me wan'   go home.

A   B A/B   E   F#m   B E

This page may be photocopied

(4.) give me such a load, me no horse with bri - dle. Day da light an' me wan' go home.

Day da light an' me wan' go home.

Day da light an' me wan' go home.

5. Five hand,____ six hand,____ sev'n hand,

5. Five hand,____ six hand,____ sev'n hand,

5. Five hand, six hand, sev'n hand,

This page may be photocopied

eight hand bunch! Day da light an' me wan' go home.

eight hand bunch! Day da light an' me wan' go home.

eight hand bunch! Day da light an' me wan' go home.

Day o, day o. Day da light an' me wan' go home.

Day o, day o. Day da light an' me wan' go home.

Day o, day o. Day da light an' me wan' go home.

Section III

Christmas and Revival Songs

12 Wash an' be Clean

RESOURCES ▶ CD1 track 12 (performance); CD2 track 13 (backing)

☐ You need to know

The 1860s in Jamaica were marked by what became known as the 'Great Revival'. This was a religious movement, led predominantly by Baptist preachers from England, during which traditional Christian beliefs were made to come alive in a new and stimulating way. Preachers told biblical stories using dramatic language and imagery, all of which was designed to enable ordinary people both to understand and to relate to the stories in a way not previously experienced. The preachers also encouraged their followers to take an active part in the religious events they mounted, by responding in chorus to their shouted and sung imprecations, and by singing well-known hymns with fervour.

The latter part of the 19th century saw the establishment of several different forms of Revivalism which continued into the 20th century. Today two principal forms survive: Revival Zion and Pocomania. These forms differ in aspects of ritual but rely on similar hymn and other musical repertoire. Drums play an important part in the accompaniment of ritual and singing.

'Wash an' be Clean' is an example of a Revivalist hymn which has been handed down over the generations. The syllable 'a' in the first line of each verse means 'to'. Biblical references include 'Bethlehem' (the birthplace of Jesus Christ), 'the Lamb' (Jesus Christ, also known as the Lamb of God), and Calvary (the place just outside Jerusalem where Christ was crucified).

☐ Warming up

- Warm up by singing the exercise below. This will stretch voices and help singers with the big leap of a major 6th at the start of the song.

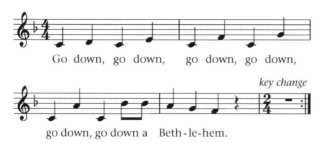

- Sing the riffs in the harmony part ('wash an' be clean') to prepare for this song. Sing with fervour, and make sure the rhythm is tight.

☐ Teaching and learning

- The melody can be taught by rote as it is so short and simple. Start by singing both verses in unison (verse 1: 'a Bethlehem'; verse 2: 'a Calvary'), aiming for a dignified and confident sound, rather like passionate hymn-singing. Make the notes full length and not *staccato*, and emphasize 'down' each time.
- Try making the word 'wash' sound more like 'warsh' than 'wosh'; also make the word 'be' lighter and sound more like 'bi' (as in '**bi**t'), and pronounce 'the' as 'de'.
- Put the melody and harmony together, mixing the available voices across the parts any way you like.
- The descant can be sung by a few voices, preferably high ones, or played on an instrument, and it must sound light and smooth. If sung, don't over-enunciate the words—it's more important to have a soft and fluty tone.

☐ Listen out

- Is the very first interval ('Go down') in tune? If not, sing the opening much more slowly, connecting the two notes; lift the arms above the head as if pulling the sound out of the top of your head.
- Is the tune strong enough? Make sure the balance is right, with enough voices on the melody.

☐ Performing

- Try an *a cappella* verse with no piano; any changed voices can create the effect of a bass-line by singing the harmony part.
- Suggested performance plan: verse 1 ('Bethlehem')— unison melody; verse 2 ('Calvary')—melody and harmony; repeat verse 1—all parts together. Follow this structure when using the backing CD.

12 Wash an' be Clean

* Verse 2 has the same words as verse 1, except that 'Bethlehem' is replaced each time with 'Calvary'.

This page may be photocopied

Go, _____ go ___ down, go down to

(2.) Cal - va - ry,

Go down a Beth-le-hem, wash an' be clean. Go wash in the blood of the

wash an' be clean, wash an' be clean. Wash in the blood of the

A   D   A   Bm   E

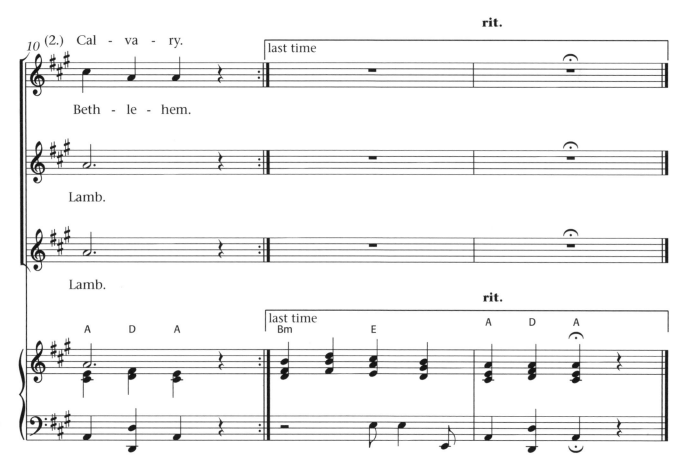

(2.) Cal - va - ry.

last time   rit.

Beth - le - hem.

Lamb.

Lamb.

A   D   A   last time   rit.
                        Bm   E   A   D   A

13 Christmas a come

RESOURCES ▶ CD1 track 13 (performance); CD2 track 14 (backing)

☐ You need to know

This cheerful Christmas song celebrates secular aspects of the religious festival, seen from the perspective of the poor, who remain a significant proportion of the Jamaican population notwithstanding the increased wealth of the middle classes today. The repeated refrain 'me wan' me lahma' can be translated as 'I want my lamé', 'lamé' being the French word for a fabric or garment woven with gold or silver (see No. 7 'Run go a Kingston'). The phrase therefore expresses the singer's desire to possess a quality garment of a distinctive nature and, by implication, of a value which she cannot afford. During verse 2 the singer further confirms her status by admitting that she has 'Not a ring to me finger' (no ring to place on her finger); and in verse 3 she confesses that she has 'Not a teet' to me mouth' (not a tooth in her mouth).

The melody, in four phrases, is delightfully simple, offering opportunities for building many layers, and inventing musical lines over the simple harmonies. The song can also be extended by inventing new phrases with which to form the basis of additional verses. One example, which works well, is 'Not a shoe to me foot'. In addition, some Jamaican choirs have taken to singing the phrase 'Not a *mm* to me *mm*' as the basis of an additional verse. This can be made humorously suggestive in the right context.

☐ Warming up

- Do some deep breathing exercises, with controlled release of air by blowing gently or hissing.
- Hum up and down the first five notes of a major scale. Change key to stretch the voices.

☐ Teaching and learning

- Teach the melody, a phrase at a time, through call and response. Point out to the singers the simplicity of the structure to help their memory: the words are paired in phrases 1 and 2, then in 3 and 4; the melody is the same shape in each phrase, and phrases 1 and 3 are identical.
- The word 'wan" should be emphasized each time to bring out the characteristic syncopated rhythm, and the singing style should be relaxed and lyrical, but cheerful.
- Sing the melody with everyone for all three verses. Note that the second half of each verse ('Pretty, pretty girl . . .') is the same. Check this is pronounced 'priddy'—no hard 't's.

- Make sure the ends of the first three phrases on 'lah-ma' are in tune (e.g. bars 4, 6, and 8)—the rising tone can often be flat.
- Now teach harmony 1—it shadows the melody. Support with an instrument if necessary.
- If changed voices are available, they should be added next, on the bass part, to underpin the harmony; it is important that they move smoothly even when the leaps between notes are larger.
- Harmony 2 can now be added—it is a simple, repetitive line, but may be the hardest to hold independently for less experienced singers. If singers struggle with this, try building up the parts starting with this line.
- A few voices can take the descant from bar 21, or it could be instrumental. This line contains more large intervals, so make sure the vocal line is smooth and in tune—be careful moving from bar 21 into 22, and from bar 25 into 26.

☐ Listen out

- Is the style relaxed and do the singers yearn for their 'lahma' (see 'You need to know', above)? To get it smooth, ask the singers to leave out the words and sing to 'na' or 'la', then add the words without breaking up the melodic line.
- What is the tuning like? If the rising tones (e.g. 'lah-ma' in bar 4) are flat, practise some of the warm-up scales, standing tall, breathing properly to support the tone, and smiling to brighten the vowel sounds.
- Can the melody be heard clearly when all parts are together? If necessary add more singers to this part and/or adjust the volume of the other parts.

☐ Performing

- Create a performance that builds up gradually. The CD recording starts with the melody only, and a mix of voices is used for each line to start with, then changed voices take the bass-line. The instrument part is added on the repeat of verse 3.
- As with all these arrangements, don't feel obliged to add all parts—just take on what is manageable so that it works confidently for your group.
- Try a completely *a cappella* version without any piano accompaniment.

13 Christmas a come

Instrument

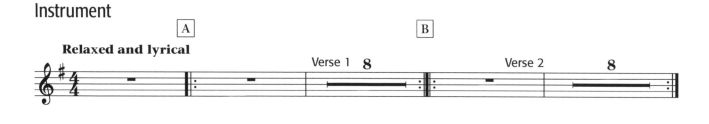

This page may be photocopied

13 Christmas a come

© Oxford University Press 2009

This page may be photocopied

This page may be photocopied

This page may be photocopied

14 Keyman

RESOURCES ▶ CD1 track 14 (performance); CD2 track 15 (backing)

☐ You need to know

This religious song refers to the biblical story of Noah and the Ark, a tale which Revivalist preachers (see No. 12 'Wash an' be Clean') would no doubt have told to their congregations with relish. According to the book of Genesis, Noah, together with his wife and sons, and the animals, survived the great flood by setting sail on a specially built ark which, as the flood waters receded, came to rest on the slopes of Ararat, one of the peaks in a remote mountain group in what is now Turkey. In 'Keyman' we are told that the animals, in their pairs, have been placed behind locked doors on the ark, presumably to ensure that they don't escape prior to the storm and that they are kept safe once the boat is on the stormy seas.

'Keyman' is typical of Jamaican religious songs in the following respects:

(a) It has a simple melody reminiscent of a hymn tune;
(b) The rhythms contained in the melody follow the crotchet beat and avoid syncopations;
(c) The melody implies a simple harmonic accompaniment created from the basic diatonic chords of G, C, and D majors (in the key of G). In traditional performance, the melody is sometimes accompanied by improvised vocal lines based on these simple harmonies.

☐ Warming up

- Do some energetic warm ups—lots of physical shakes.
- Loosen tongues by reciting 'the lips, the teeth, the tip of the tongue' repeatedly, getting faster.
- Sing the exercise below, starting at any comfortable pitch, raising it several times to stretch voices.

do be do be do be do be   do be do be do

☐ Teaching and learning

- Start with the chorus (bars 11–18). Teach the two simple melody phrases 'Keyman lock the door an' gone' in bars 13–14 and 17–18. Now sing 'Keyman, Keyman . . .' in bars 11–12 and 15–16 and get the group to answer with their phrases.
- Divide the singers into two equal groups—one group joins you with 'Keyman, Keyman . . .', and the other responds with 'Keyman lock . . .' as above. Swap the groups over and repeat.
- Learn the melody for the verse (bars 2–10), noting that

bars 3–4 match bars 7–8. Make sure the singers support the top E in bar 9.

- Sing the whole song in unison, dividing the chorus as above for variety. The words should be clear and the style light and *staccato*.
- Continue to work on the verse, adding the bass part first. This follows the simple harmonic pattern and is quite repetitive; the last phrase (bars 9–10) matches the melody rhythm so that all voices emphasize the revelation that the 'Keyman lock the door an' gone'!
- The harmony part should be taken by the most confident voices. It has a melodic quality of its own but occasionally clashes with the melody in passing (e.g. bar 3 beat 2; bar 4 beat 3).
- The descant, which is sung to 'ah', will sound smoother than the other parts.
- Next move on to the chorus. Note the use of typical Jamaican syncopated rhythms in the harmony and bass parts in bars 11–12 and 15–16. The intention here is to provide some gentle rhythmic energy to keep the pace going without the accompaniment. Keep these bars subtle so that they don't dominate the 'straight' melody.
- Put the whole chorus section together, slowly and carefully, to check the rhythms and the tuning, particularly in bar 16. The ending, from bar 19, is the same as this section.
- Sing the whole song, starting with the parts that are confident. This might be unison first section with harmony chorus, or vice versa, until all the parts are ready. Note that chord symbols are provided in the *a cappella* sections to support the voices should this be necessary.

☐ Listen out

- Are the rhythms secure with a good feeling of pulse? Encourage this by walking on the spot while singing, listening carefully to the regular piano pattern.
- Does the chorus work without the piano? Check the syncopated rhythms and the pitches for accuracy in bars 11–12 and 15–16; support with chords if necessary.
- Are the descant singers getting the large leap in bar 17 accurately? If not, improve pitching by singing the three notes on 'Keyman lock' slowly, repeating many times, gradually getting faster; then extend this to 'Keyman lock the door', aiming for 'door' each time.
- What dynamic contrasts do you want? Make sure everyone sings what is marked, or whatever you decide if it is different.

▢ Performing

- This song could be sung through any number of times, adding a part each time, and could even be sung unaccompanied. The descant could be played by an instrument.
- CD performance plan: melody only to bar 10, then melody, harmony, and bass from bar 11; all parts on repeat, and through to the end.
- When using the backing CD, repeat bars 3–18 once only.
- You could try a simpler version with melody and more basic harmony, possibly with some improvisation from backing voices (see 'You need to know', above).

14 Keyman

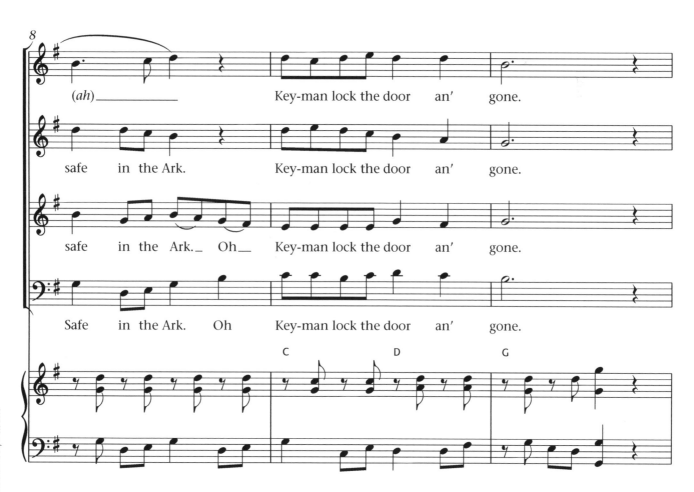

This page may be photocopied

14. Keyman **69**

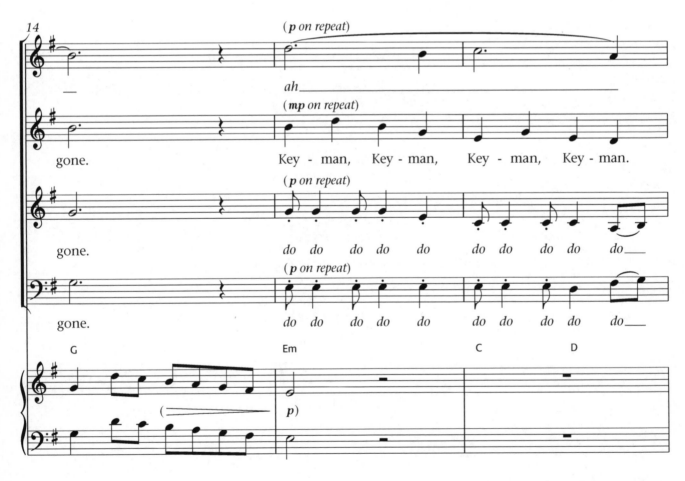

This page may be photocopied

This page may be photocopied

© Oxford University Press 2009

15 Born to rule

RESOURCES ▶ CD1 track 15 (performance); CD2 track 16 (backing)

☐ You need to know

The simple yet captivating melody of 'Born to rule' is typical of Jamaican traditional music in its use of a repeated ♪ ♩ figure, which is a simple form of syncopation. This figure forms the basis of the first three bars of the tune. The syncopated figure is then discarded in favour of the 'on the beat' rhythms of the last two phrases of the melody. The song is unusual in that each verse is six bars, rather than four or eight bars, long. It is arranged for up to six parts, in different combinations to give it variety, and to create a full and joyous sound for the 'What a joy!' section. The structure is **A B A C A Coda**.

The words to which this traditional melody is set are by Louise Bennett who, until her death in 2006, led the movement which sought to preserve Jamaica's traditional music and language. Bennett recorded many Jamaican songs (including No. 10 'Brown Girl in the Ring') and wrote several books of poems which explore a variety of Jamaican themes through the medium of the national language. In the case of 'Born to rule', the phoneticizations stem from Jamaican language usage. They are 'de' (pronounced 'dee' and a version of 'the' in English), 'eart'' (earth), 'worl'' (world), and 'deh' (there).

☐ Warming up

- Practise standing tall and breathing deeply. Place both hands over the middle of the stomach and, while breathing in slowly, pull the hands outwards, imagining a big barrel of air in front of you. Breathe out, doing the reverse, keeping the shoulders down.
- Sing Ex. 1 at the foot of the page, changing key to stretch the voices across the full range.

☐ Teaching and learning

- First learn the melody of the 'A' section; bars 11–16 are a repeat of bars 5–10. Sing all three verses warmly and with clear diction.
- Now work on putting all parts in the 'A' section together. Start with the simple bass part—sing the words even though they belong to verse 3. Add as many of the harmony parts as you can, starting with the top line, and practise them with the bass part until it sounds confident and together.
- The 'B' section (bars 17–23) comes next. The harmony part shadows the melody up to bar 20, and moves with the bass part in bars 22–3. Practise it with both the other lines separately before putting them all together. Make sure 'What a joy!' is strong in the lower two parts

even though the rhythm is different.
- The parts switch roles in the 'C' section, with the bass part on the tune. Practise the upper parts together slowly, making sure they move together on the beat until bar 29, and aren't tempted to 'swing' with the basses.
- When putting the whole song together, check carefully that the joins between sections are confident—every singer must know which note they are moving to. Practise moving from bar 23 and bar 30 back to bar 5, as there is no piano break to give singers time to think and prepare.
- Finally practise the Coda—singers must know where they are getting their notes from so that the chords are confident and tidy.

☐ Listen out

- Is everyone confident about the structure of the song? Talk through the geography of the song, singing the few bars around the joins if necessary. See the performance plan below.
- Are the words pronounced as indicated in 'You need to know', above? Read through the words to check that everyone is doing the same.
- What is the balance like when all the parts are together? The melody could be obscured—check this and redistribute voices if required.

☐ Performing

- Performance plan: 'A' section (verse 1)—melody only (upper or mixed voices); 'B' section—all three parts, *a cappella*, or with piano for support; 'A' section (verse 2)—melody plus harmony (one, two, or three parts as appropriate); 'C' section—all three parts, *a cappella*, or with piano for support; 'A' section (verse 3)—all parts; Coda.

Ex. 1

Born to rule de eart', born to rule de eart',

born to rule de eart', born to rule__ de
key change

eart'. What a joy!

15 Born to rule

Words: Louise Bennett
Music: Jamaican trad.
arr. Michael Burnett and Peter Hunt

This page may be photocopied

This page may be photocopied

This page may be photocopied

This page may be photocopied

This page may be photocopied

Music © Oxford University Press 2009; Text © Louise Bennett Coverley Estate, Canada

Section IV

Rastafarian Songs

16 Mount Zion

RESOURCES ▶ CD1 track 16 (performance); CD2 track 17 (backing)

☐ You need to know

Rastafarians belong to a religious cult which was formed in Jamaica during the first half of the 20th century. Rastafarian beliefs are partly derived from Christianity, and the cult's rituals focus upon the exile of their ancestors, and other consequences of the transatlantic slave trade in Africans (see 'Jamaican Song and Dance'). For this reason, Rastafarians living in Jamaica believe that Africa is their spiritual homeland. Indeed, their texts and songs often refer to an imagined journey back to that continent and to Ethiopia, the African country which symbolizes paradise and is often referred to as 'Zion', or 'Mount Zion', by Rastafarians. In biblical terms Zion represents a place where happiness can be achieved and suffering can be brought to an end.

'Mount Zion' is a song true to the Rastafarian tradition, and one which sets the religion in its context of poverty. For, until quite recently, some Jamaicans in country districts would have viewed having a pair of shoes as a luxury. Here, the singer expresses the belief that everyone in the symbolic paradise of Ethiopia will possess shoes and that he, or she, will 'put on me shoe' to walk 'all over Mount Zion'. The reference to 'I an' I' in the words of the song is typically Rastafarian. Practitioners of this form of religion believe that they are at one with God (called 'Jah' by Rastafarians), and they express this by referring to the two elements of the 'oneness': 'I [the human] an' I [the God-derived]'.

☐ Warming up

- Warm up with some gentle arpeggio exercises.
- Sing the exercise below. Start slowly and *legato*, then try it *staccato* and quicker, raising the pitch to stretch voices.

- Sing 'She'll be coming round the mountain when she comes' if you know it! The melody shapes are similar.

☐ Teaching and learning

- Everyone should learn the melody first; make the words very clear by keeping the sound *staccato*. Soften 'got to' to 'godda', and 'go **to** Zion' to 'go **da** Zion'; nothing must sound too English.
- In bar 9 stress the word '**ov**er' to emphasize this characteristic Jamaican rhythm.
- Learn harmony 2 next; sing the long notes in bars 3–8 quietly and smoothly, then give more energy from bar 9, to match the melody. Enjoy the cheeky answering phrases in bars 10 and 11 and make sure they are in tune—jumping a small interval singing *staccato* can result in poor pitching.
- Put these parts together, using all singers if possible, divided equally.
- When these parts are confident look at harmony 1; it is repetitive and well supported by the piano part, which should therefore be used if possible. Make sure singers breathe in good time so that the upbeat entries aren't late.
- Put all three parts together slowly at first, making sure they move together.

☐ Listen out

- Is the ensemble good? The trickiest place is bar 8 where the melody has a slurred note which could rush; harmony 1 has an upbeat which could be late; and harmony 2 has a different rhythm on the main beats! It's worth tackling this bar slowly, encouraging everyone to aim for 'walk' in bar 9 absolutely together.
- Are bars 9 and 14*b*–15 together? Everyone sings unison rhythms here to emphasize the important words. Try mixing everyone up and sing through without a conductor.
- Are the chord changes in tune? Check particularly bars 6 and 11, where the As in the chord of F may go flat. Avoid this by getting singers to smile as they sing, to brighten the vowels.

☐ Performing

- It is customary in songs that express belief or desire, like many spirituals, to add words to extend it. Try making up your own words, e.g. 'I got a song . . . gonna sing all over . . .' or 'I got some news . . . gonna shout all over . . .'.
- Try making up ostinato patterns for high-, medium-, and low-pitched hand drums—listen to the backing CD for ideas of how to make them sound typically Rastafarian. Adding these will bring extra colour to a performance.
- Suggested performance plan: melody; melody and harmony 1 or 2; all parts.
- When using the backing CD, sing through three times.

16 Mount Zion

17 Back to Ethiopia

RESOURCES ▶ CD1 track 17 (performance); CD2 track 18 (backing)

▢ You need to know

This beautiful song is typical of a number of Jamaican traditional religious melodies: it is in a major key and simply structured, yet it can convey a real sense of profundity and sadness if performed with dignity and at a deliberate tempo. (No. 19 'Peace an' love' and No. 20 'Rivers of Babylon' have similar characteristics.) Again, the theme of 'Back to Ethiopia' is the Rastafarian belief that this African country represents the true homeland of those whose ancestors were captured, brought to Jamaica, and enslaved. Hence the reference in the song to the performer's desire to be 'taken back' to Ethiopia and the affirmation of religious belief in the refrain 'Oh yes Rastafari, oh yes'.

The simple structure of 'Back to Ethiopia' is defined by its five short phrases, each two bars long. The first three phrases use the same repeated rhythmic pattern. This pattern opens with the typically Jamaican syncopation ♩ ♪♩. (see, for example, No. 15 'Born to rule'). Then, in a manner redolent of Jamaican traditional melodies, the song ends with two phrases that contrast strongly with those preceding them. Each of these phrases begins with a sustained, bar-long note as opposed to the syncopations which begin the first three phrases. And, as if to give the song new rhythmic life, a second syncopation ♪♩ ♪ occurs during phrase 4 to the words 'yes Rastafari'.

▢ Warming up

- Start with some gentle stretching exercises, raising the arms above the head to lift the rib cage.
- Breathe in slowly for a count of four, hold it, then hiss slowly, remaining tall without shoulders collapsing.
- Sing the exercise below, with a clear 'k' placed on the fourth beat, but in one breath to give it a sense of shape and direction. Raise the pitch gradually to G major to cover the range required for the song.
- If the pitch drops as the notes rise, get singers to put out their hands, palms down at about waist height, and gradually push down (as if pressing on a table) as the notes go higher.

▢ Teaching and learning

- Encourage singers to imagine that they have a strong desire to be somewhere better and safer.
- Learn the melody by rote, using the breath control and pitch awareness exercises from the warm up to keep it musical and in tune. Observing the dynamic markings will encourage singers to express the song musically.
- The word 'land' should be pronounced 'lan", and 'Rastafari' pronounced 'Rastafar**eye**'.
- In contrast to the melody, the harmony part is not syncopated in bars 5–10 and is in contrary motion with the tune. Learn it one phrase at a time and make sure it never dominates the melody.

▢ Listen out

- Is everyone singing in tune? The rising nature of the melody, and the step up a tone from bar 6 into bar 7, might cause flatness, so make sure the vowel sound is bright and, if necessary, repeat some of the warm-up work.
- Are the singers finishing the phrases together with a clear but gentle consonant on the fourth beat (bars 6, 8, 10, and 14)? Make sure you indicate this clearly when conducting; repeat the warm-up exercise if necessary.
- Is the harmony line supporting the melody? If it is too strong, consider a different balance of voices between parts.

▢ Performing

- The most important thing is that the melody is sung musically, with the appropriate feeling; it could be performed without the harmony.
- The performance must be very expressive, and end very quietly.
- Try adding the harmony on a violin or viola instead of voices.
- Try making up ostinato patterns for high-, medium-, and low-pitched hand drums—listen to the backing CD for ideas of how to make them sound typically Rastafarian. This is a gentle and expressive song, so make sure they don't overpower the melody.
- The CD performance features melody only, harmony only, then both parts together.
- When using the backing CD, sing three times.

17 Back to Ethiopia

Lyrical and rueful

Melody

Harmony

Lyrical and rueful

Piano

Take me back to E-thi - o - pia land, take me back to E-thi - o - pia land,

Take me back to E-thi - o - pia land, oh_ take_____ me back. mm_

This page may be photocopied

This page may be photocopied

18 Zion me wan' go home

RESOURCES ▶ CD1 track 18 (performance)

☐ You need to know

This is another song that refers to Zion. To Rastafarians, Zion represents, in religious terms, a place of solace and redemption; in geographical terms it represents the African country of Ethiopia. So when the performer of the song tells us that he or she wants to 'go home', it is to Ethiopia that the singer desires to go. The melancholy melody of 'Zion me wan' go home' expresses something of the sense of longing felt by Rastafarians for this distant place where their present suffering will be relieved. The melody's use of the Aeolian mode, with its minor 3rd and 7th (and minor 6th implied in the accompanying harmonies), helps provide some of this sense of melancholy, although the mode is otherwise not commonly used in Jamaican traditional music.

During verse 2 the singer mentions Africa, the continent from which his or her ancestors were brought on the slave ships prior to the British abolition of the transatlantic trade in Africans in 1807. The word 'fe' means 'to' in this context. Drumming was one of the musical skills brought by the slaves to Jamaica and, because of this, drums play an important part in Rastafarian ritual (see p. xi). Some suggested drum patterns are provided as ostinato accompaniments; of these patterns, the bass drum rhythm in particular is fundamental to Rastafarian music.

☐ Warming up

- After some breathing exercises, sing the scale of the Aeolian mode (see below) to the solfège names or any vowel sound, or hum.

- To help listening and tuning, repeat the exercise and invite each singer to stop and sustain any note until a cluster is built up.
- Repeat this, but ask everyone to choose note 1, 3, 5, or 8—the tonic chord of this song.
- Walk slowly on the spot to establish a pulse, then gently chant the words of the first phrase; turn it into a canon

by getting a second group to echo the first, starting when the first group reaches bar 2.

☐ Teaching and learning

- Teach the melody by rote, call and response style; make sure the very first leap is in tune, and ensure the falling phrases (bars 3 and 4) don't go flat.
- Look at the bass part next; it shares some notes with the melody (check the tuning of these) and underpins the harmony in bars 3–4.
- Now add the harmony parts—these fill out the chords. Harmony 2 is the easiest to learn as it only has three notes.
- Make sure singers separate the final 'go home' in bars 2 and 6.
- In verses 2 and 3, the rhythm should be adjusted in bars 1 and 5 to fit with the words: all parts should follow the rhythm given in 'Other verses'.
- This song is best learnt with a leader to facilitate the learning, rather than having a conductor, so that singers really listen to each other for ensemble and tuning.

☐ Listen out

- Is the melody in tune? Danger points are the opening rising 5th, the rising tones on 'me wan' go', and the falling minor 3rds in bars 3 (C–A) and 4 (F–D). Support these moments with good breathing, lift the cheeks to brighten the sound, and listen carefully.
- Is everyone moving together in bars 1 and 5? Chant the words to help the rhythm become really ingrained.

☐ Performing

- The CD performance builds up the parts one at a time: verse 1—melody; verse 2—melody and bass; verse 3—melody, bass, and harmony 2; back to verse 1—all parts, twice through.
- Verses with melody only can be sung by all voices, a small group, or a soloist.
- Drums can be added as suggested, as can chords on guitar or keyboard.
- The final verse can be gentle or strong—ask the singers how they want it to end.

18 Zion me wan' go home

Other verses

2. Af - ri - ca me wan' fe go.___
3. E - thi - o - pia land fe go.___

Suggested drum patterns

This page may be photocopied

19 Peace an' love

RESOURCES ▶ CD1 track 19 (performance)

☐ You need to know

'Peace an' love' is a particularly well-known Rastafarian song in Jamaica. Indeed, the song's wistful melody and words have found a place in the repertoire of other religious groups. As in No. 18 'Zion me wan' go home', the drums play an important role when a song such as 'Peace an' love' is performed during Rastafarian ritual. Some suggested accompaniments are provided here and the mesmeric effect of the repeated quavers on the first beat of each bar of the song is an important element in the creation of a sense of Rastafarian musical style. The tempo of performance should be deliberate, without being too slow, and the manner dignified.

The theme of 'Peace an' love' is the Rastafarian conviction that Ethiopia is the spiritual homeland of members of this cult (see p. xi). In biblical terms Ethiopia is often referred to as 'Zion', and Rastafarians talk of making the journey to Ethiopia (or Zion) to seek release from their present suffering. This song raises the issue of members of a Rastafarian family not wishing to make the journey, for whatever reason. So if 'your mother' or 'your father' or 'your sister' won't go, the singer will leave his or her 'peace an' love' with you. One of the ironies of Rastafarianism is that it is a peace-loving cult, despite its origins partly as a response to the centuries-long violence perpetrated on the ancestors of members of the cult by the English slave traders.

☐ Warming up

- Encourage the singers to stand very still, eyes closed, breathing slowly and more deeply than normal. On a given signal they should breathe in, then gently hum any note, making it last only as long as the outgoing breath; this should be totally relaxed.
- Chant 'Peace an' love' repeatedly, to the opening rhythm of the melody, on any comfortable low note; there should be a two-beat breath in between each repetition. Get singers to practise using all of their air on the long note, giving it a focused but quiet tone. Extend this by introducing the second phrase (bars 4–6).

☐ Teaching and learning

- After the warm-up chant, teach the melody up to bar 8.
- The second half (the 'verse', bars 8–16), has the same melody but with faster rhythms to fit the words 'An' if your mother won' go'. Try this next.

- Now learn the bass part—it mostly fits between the melody phrases, which makes it quite easy to hear. Check the tuning of the rising intervals in bars 5 and 13.
- Harmony 1 echoes the melody, so tackle this part next. Notice that the notes are different in bars 13–14 compared to bars 5–6; these higher notes will need supporting with good breath, and should be sung with a floating head-voice tone. Check the move from 'peace an'' to 'love' in bars 6–7 and 14–15—it's a rising tone.
- Finally add harmony 2, making sure that, when it rises to the same note as harmony 1 (G in bars 2 and 10), these parts are in unison.
- When the parts are put together, encourage the singers to sing with expression and give shape to the lines; the regular crotchet melody could sound dull without some natural inflection. Speak the lyrics to decide which words should be stressed.

☐ Listen out

- Does the music move together and sound expressive? Make sure the singers are aware of the phrase lengths and where the lines are going.
- Are the final notes of phrases the right length? Check that the singers on the melody part are holding the semibreves on 'love' sufficiently long (as in the warm up), but that the lower parts stop their crotchets in bars 8 and 10 at the right time to allow the melody to come through clearly.

☐ Performing

- The CD performance features all parts from the beginning for all three verses. For verse 3 changed voices are added on the melody—this adds a different tone and some depth for variety. Another option would be to add a part on each repetition.
- The CD performance also features the high drum rhythm from the suggested percussion backing. The most important rhythm is the two quavers on the first beat, but add all the parts if you can.
- On the final repeat add a low G to the bass part (last note) to give the performance a strong ending.
- Dynamics are left to the performers: such a graceful and poignant song needs little fuss, but some variation is effective. Try some really *pianissimo* singing.

19 Peace an' love

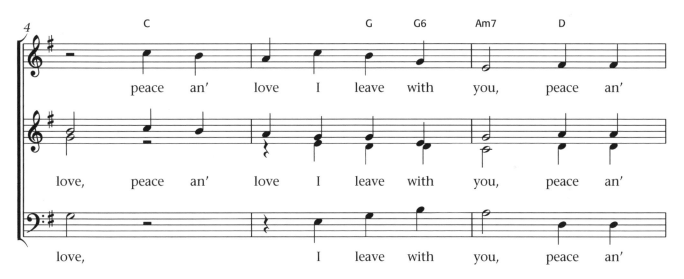

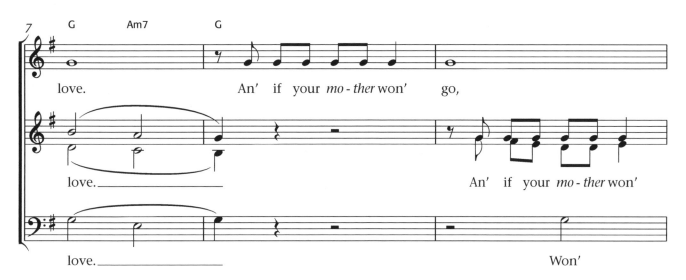

* Other verses: replace 'mother' each time with 'father' for verse 2 and 'sister' for verse 3.

This page may be photocopied

Suggested drum patterns

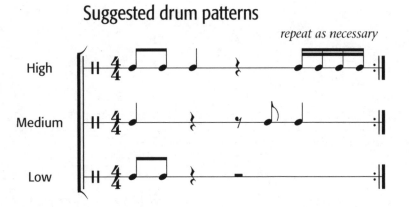

This page may be photocopied

Section V

Popular Songs

20 Rivers of Babylon

RESOURCES ▶ CD1 track 20 (performance); CD2 track 19 (backing)

☐ You need to know

'Rivers of Babylon' was first made famous when it was recorded, in 1972, by the Melodians, a Jamaican rock steady band influenced by the Rastafarian religion. A version of the song was then released by Boney M, two of whose band members are from Jamaica, in 1978. This recording of 'Rivers of Babylon' was on a single containing another well-known Jamaican song, 'Brown Girl in the Ring' (No. 10). Nearly two million copies of Boney M's version of 'Rivers of Babylon' were subsequently sold in the UK.

'Rivers of Babylon' takes as its theme Psalm 137, which tells of the exile of the Jewish people after the Babylonian conquest of Jerusalem in 586BC. For Rastafarians, the parallel between the exile of the Jews and the exile of their African ancestors to Jamaica as a result of the slave trade is of immense significance. The Africans were indeed 'carried away [into] captivity' by 'the wicked' English traders; and they were indeed taken from their homeland (referred to here as 'Zion') to a 'strange land' (Jamaica) where they suffered the cruelties of enslavement. This has led Rastafarians to describe Jamaica as 'Babylon', a place of suffering equivalent to the Babylon known to the exiled Jews. The reference in 'Rivers of Babylon' to King Alpha is typical of Rastafarian practice. Members of the cult believe that Emperor Haile Selassie 1 of Ethiopia, who died in 1975, is Jah (their God incarnate), and 'King Alpha' is used by Rastafarians as an alternative name for him.

☐ Warming up

- Sing up and down the first five notes of the major scale to 'ba-da', or any scat syllables. Sing in a relaxed way, and focus on bright tuning as the notes rise. Change key to stretch the voices.
- Sing the popular Scottish song 'My bonny lies over the ocean' if you know it! The opening phrase is good preparation for this song.

☐ Teaching and learning

- Everyone should sing the melody and enjoy it. Pay attention to phrase endings, and check the rhythm in bar 8 and bars 15–16.
- The second-time bar (10*b*) can be sung as written or an octave higher to suit the singer(s).
- Build up the chorus parts in the first section (bars 1–10), starting with the soprano and alto parts. The sound should be quiet and sustained, but with a short '-lon' (or 'down', *etc.*) at the end of each phrase.

- The bass part adds some rhythm and should be quiet and focused. Articulate the 'do' at the front of the mouth for a gently percussive sound.
- If there are enough singers, add the tenor part next, ensuring that the last two notes of each phrase (C and D) are in tune.
- Rehearse the chorus parts together to bar 10, then add the melody and descant. These parts can be sung by a soloist or a small group, and the descant could also be instrumental. Soloists on the melody can be freer with rhythm and expression.
- Look at the chorus parts for bars 11–18 next. The lines are kept simple to ensure a smooth sound, and this acts as a cushion for the more rhythmic melody. Put this section together as quickly as possible; the piano covers the harmony, so leave out any parts you don't have the singers for!
- Rehearse the crescendo and decrescendo in bars 13–14, and the crescendo in bars 16–17; these subtle changes will add some interest and energy to the backing chorus.
- Now learn the Coda; it starts with unison chorus parts, then breaks into harmony for the cadence.

☐ Listen out

- Is the melody strong enough? The backing chorus could be overwhelming so make sure the vocal sound is focused and quiet—clarity of words is not important here.
- Are the chorus parts in tune? Ensure the sopranos and altos are hitting their notes on the last beat of bar 3 (and similar places); the rich harmony here could put singers off, especially with the small leap to these notes.
- If a group is singing the melody, are the singers matching each other? Check they are breathing in good time so that the starts and ends of the phrases are together.

☐ Performing

- The melody must be strong. You could start with everyone singing the melody, and then repeat with a soloist accompanied by the backing chorus.
- Add the descant, either vocally or instrumentally, on the final repeat.
- The backing CD presents a fuller accompaniment for this song to liven up performances.

20 Rivers of Babylon

Words: Psalm 137
Music: Jamaican trad.
arr. Michael Burnett and Peter Hunt

This page may be photocopied

This page may be photocopied

This page may be photocopied

21 One love/People Get Ready

RESOURCES ▶ CD1 track 21 (performance); CD2 track 20 (backing)

☐ You need to know

Bob Marley (1945–81) is possibly the most famous of all reggae artists. 'One love/People Get Ready' was released on the *Exodus* album by Bob Marley and the Wailers in 1977. It is a reworking of the Curtis Mayfield song 'People Get Ready', setting new lyrics to the original melody and accompaniment. *Exodus* was recorded at the Island Records studio in London. It was one of the first reggae albums to be recorded with high quality sound engineering, and was instrumental in establishing Bob Marley as an internationally renowned reggae star.

The course of Bob Marley's life changed when he converted to Rastafarianism. He began writing songs that expressed Rasta sentiments, and actively promoted peace and tolerance among West Indian peoples at a time when his home country of Jamaica was experiencing gang warfare and rioting. Marley maintained that communities should find a common ground in order to live in amity. In this song he argues that we can promote equality if we 'get together' and put aside individuality. He asks us to fight 'Holy Armageddon' and prepare for 'when the man comes', a reference to the second coming of the Saviour that will mark the end of the world.

☐ Warming up

- Stand the singers in a circle and put on a reggae track. Get everyone to step and clap along to the music, with steps on the main beats and claps on the off beats. Experiment with fading the music out and back in again, so that singers have to focus on maintaining a steady beat.
- Now speak the rhythm of bars 5–14 over a steady pulse. Lean on the words with exclamation marks.

☐ Teaching and learning

- This song is easily taught by rote. Start by teaching the chorus (bars 5–14) to the choir, in this order: soprano 1; baritone; alto; soprano 2. The alto part could also be sung by tenors, in which case give the soprano 2 part to the altos.
- Practise bars 10–12 slowly—the rhythm is more challenging here and needs to be together.
- The singers should place consonants gently and exactly together on the fourth beats of bars (e.g. bar 5).
- Once the singers have learnt their parts fluently, add the 'step–clap' pulse to keep the parts together and to add some bounce.

- Next add in the lead part for bars 5–14, which can be sung by any voice type. Ask singers to focus on making this into a dialogue between the lead and the backing vocals, again ensuring that the words of the backing are perfectly together.
- Now turn to the rest of the song (from bar 14). The lead vocal can sing his/her part freely and expressively, but the backing vocals need to be really secure and rhythmic for this to work. It may be worth running this section through several times, with the soloist speaking the words, in order to coordinate it with the other parts.
- Sing bars 29–32 repeatedly until everyone is moving together, especially on 'give' in bar 32. Once this is confident, sing the whole song through from start to finish.

☐ Listen out

- Is the balance between the choir parts (backing vocals) right? Mix the group up so that, as far as possible, each singer is standing next to someone singing a different part. Encourage them to modify the dynamic at which they are singing so that no single voice stands out.
- Can the soloist be heard? Check the balance of the chorus with the solo verses. Ask individuals to stop singing and listen to the choir to see which parts should be singing louder or softer.
- Is the ending together? The last bar can be sung slowly and out of tempo; singers should feel how much to slow down by really listening, like a gospel choir.

☐ Performing

- This piece should be a heartfelt acclamation of the value of harmony and community spirit. Make the performance reflect on the importance of finding ways for different communities to live in peace.
- There is some variety in the scoring, which will create dynamic contrast, but it is effective when the chorus is sung loudly, and the verse is sung quieter and in a more intimate way. Encourage the soloist to sing directly to the audience as if delivering a special message.
- Encourage the soloist to be expressive with the melody: it is not essential to stick rigidly to the notation. Listen to the CD performance for inspiration.
- The backing CD presents a fuller accompaniment for this song to liven up performances. When using this, sing the last four bars three times, with the final bar (unaccompanied) much slower.

21 One love/People Get Ready

One love: Bob Marley
People Get Ready: Curtis Mayfield
arr. Rebecca Berkley

One love! one heart! Let's get to-ge - ther and

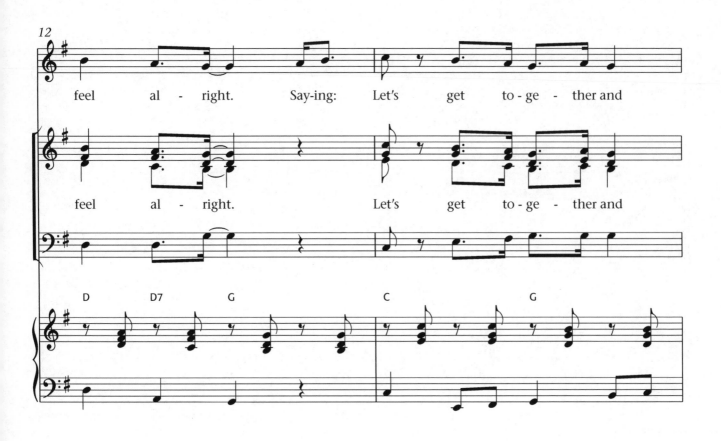

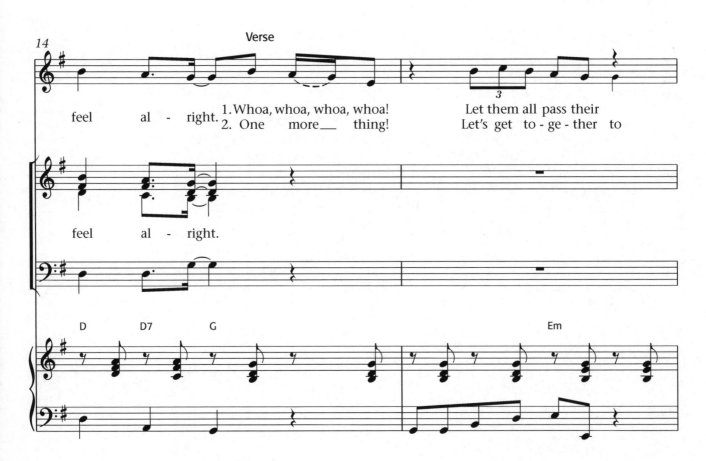

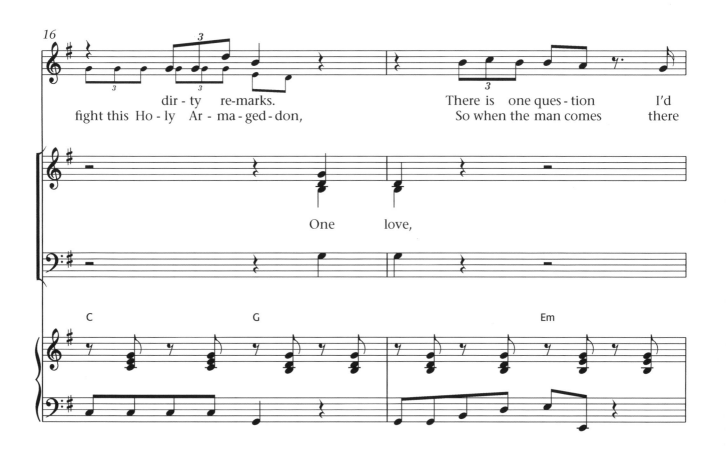

16

dir-ty re-marks.
fight this Ho - ly Ar - ma - ged - don,

There is one ques - tion   I'd
So when the man comes   there

One   love,

C   G   Em

18

real-ly love to ask: Is there a place_ for the   hope-less sin - ner Who has
will be no, no doom.   Have pi - ty on those whose chan   -   ces grow thin-ner, There ain't

one heart,
one song,

C   D   G   Em   C   G

29

thanks and praise to the Lord and I will feel al - right. Say-ing:

thanks and praise to the Lord and I will feel al - right.

C   G   D   D7   G

31

repeat ad lib. | last time

Let's get to-ge - ther and feel al - right. Give feel al - right.

Let's get to-ge - ther and feel al - right. Give feel al - right.

C   G   D   D7   G

repeat ad lib. | last time
D   D7   G

ad lib.

21 One love/People Get Ready

Vocal score

One love: Bob Marley
People Get Ready: Curtis Mayfield
arr. Rebecca Berkley

22 Island in the Sun

RESOURCES ▶ CD1 track 22 (performance); CD2 track 21 (backing)

You need to know

'Island in the Sun' is sometimes called the national anthem of the Caribbean because its lyrics could apply to many of the islands in the region. In addition, the song's catchy melody, with its memorable chorus, taps into an apparently regional style which has great tourist appeal. However, the composer and first performer of 'Island in the Sun' was the Jamaican–American Harry Belafonte and the clear-cut, repeated syncopations in the melody line (most often ♪♩♪ or ♩♪♩.) are redolent of Jamaican traditional music. So it seems reasonable to claim the melody as of Jamaican descent. The lyrics of the song were written by Irving Burgess, another American with links to the Caribbean (his mother was from Barbados).

Belafonte's 'Island in the Sun' was first released, as a single, in 1957. The song was featured on the soundtrack of the film *Island in the Sun*, released in the same year. By this time Harry Belafonte was known as a calypso singer, and this term was often applied to songs such as 'Island in the Sun'. However, calypso is actually the national dance song of Trinidad and Tobago, and true calypsos tend to be more complex rhythmically, and harmonically, than these songs. The national dance song of Jamaica is mento (see p. x).

Warming up

- Begin by humming up and down a C major scale to 'nah' and 'noo'. Make sure the higher notes have the same warmth and support as the lower notes.
- Sing the exercise below in any key, with singers picking any note. Concentrate on tuning and moving together.

Teaching and learning

- Teach the melody to all singers, phrase by phrase. It should be relaxed and have a slight lilt. Make sure that singers only breathe at the ends of phrases and that the words are clear. Practise the crescendo in bars 24–6; it should be smooth and well supported.

- You could try softening the words by singing 'ma' instead of 'my', 'de' instead of 'the', and 'arl' instead of 'all' and '**al**ways'. You could also drop the 'g' of 'shining'.
- Now teach the alto part in bars 11–18, and then fit the parts together; those on the tune could hum their line while the altos sing out.
- Tackle bars 29–39 next. Like the warm-up exercise, the parts move together rhythmically here.
- Return to bars 19–26. The rhythm of the baritone part is tricky, so start by getting the baritones to speak the words while the other parts hum. Once this is confident, add the baritone melody. Take care that the falling notes at the ends of phrases, e.g. bars 20 and 22, are accurate.
- Put all parts together and sing through.

Listen out

- Is the sound relaxed? Make sure the repeated quavers (e.g. bars 5 and 8) aren't rushed.
- Is everyone singing soulfully about their island? The words should be clear, and the rhythms should sound confident.
- Is the baritone line in bars 19–26 confident? It should sound like one voice so practise it slowly, or consider giving it to one singer. Check the large leaps in bars 24–5.
- Does the music flow? Sing in phrases, using the words as a guide, and check that singers only breathe at the commas.

Performing

- A good performance will be shaped like an arc, with a gentle beginning and ending, and a more assertive central section. Take care that each phrase from bar 33 is softer than the one that precedes it.
- Less confident groups can sing the alternative ending from bar 29 (p. 117), which has simpler vocal lines and a piano accompaniment for support.
- The backing CD presents a fuller accompaniment for this song to liven up performances. Choirs have the option of using either version of bars 29–40 with the backing.

22 Island in the Sun

Irving Burgess and Harry Belafonte
arr. Kevin Stannard

Soprano: This is my is - land in the sun,_ where my peo-ple have toiled since time be - gun._ I may sail_ on ma-ny a sea,_ her shores will al-ways be home to me.

* An alternative performance option with accompaniment from bar 29 is given on page 117.

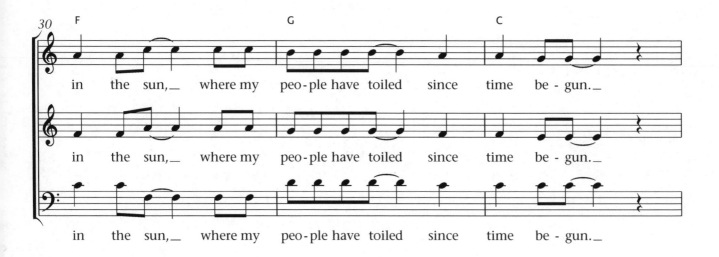

in the sun,— where my peo-ple have toiled since time be-gun.—

in the sun,— where my peo-ple have toiled since time be-gun.—

in the sun,— where my peo-ple have toiled since time be-gun.—

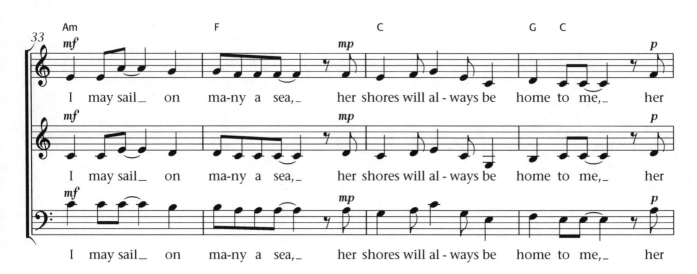

I may sail— on ma-ny a sea,— her shores will al-ways be home to me,— her

I may sail— on ma-ny a sea,— her shores will al-ways be home to me,— her

I may sail— on ma-ny a sea,— her shores will al-ways be home to me,— her

shores will al-ways be home to me.

shores will al-ways be home to me.

shores will al-ways be home to me.

Alternative performance option from bar 29

23 My boy lollipop

RESOURCES ▶ CD1 track 23 (performance); CD2 track 22 (backing)

You need to know

'My boy lollipop' was recorded by Millie Small in 1964 and sold 7 million copies, making it one of the biggest-selling ska hits of all time. It was the first major hit for the Island Records label for whom the vast majority of reggae stars like Bob Marley and Jimmy Cliff recorded in the 1960s–80s.

This song is in the ska style, a type of pop music that mixes elements of mento with rhythm and blues. Ska was the principal popular style in Jamaica in the 1960s and then spread to the UK (and US) in the 1970s and 1980s, where '2-tone' or mod bands like The Specials and Madness created a UK ska sound. Ska has an upbeat tempo with a walking bass and off-beat guitar chords or 'chops'. The term is reputed to have been coined by musicians to describe the 'ska, ska' sound made by the rhythm guitarist. This song also owes much to the all-female close harmony groups of the late 1950s and 1960s like The Shirelles.

Warming up

- Start with a physical warm up to loosen the upper body. Ask singers to imagine that they have a pencil on the end of their chins and to draw circles, squares, and figures of eight of various sizes. Massage the face, and do a silent scream with the mouth open wide, followed immediately by scrunching the face up.
- Raise the pulse with some simple physical activity. Play a suitable up-tempo track on CD to accompany moves such as walking on the spot, swinging the arms, and step and clap patterns.
- Sing the exercise below, starting on any note. Move up the scale for each repetition to stretch the voices, and make sure tongues are mobile and loose on the 'l's. Add some twisty dance movements on the spot to get into the groove.

Easy ska swing

Lol-li-pop, lol-li-pop, lol-li, lol-li, lol-li-pop.

Teaching and learning

- Teach the opening melody to all singers, in a slow tempo, and sing phrases in pairs, e.g. 'My boy lollipop'—'you make my heart go giddy up'. Make sure that the singers observe the rests accurately and clip the final consonant short.

- To help brighten the tone, you could try adding a slight American accent. Singers can articulate the pairs of notes like 'so' and 'desire' at the ends of phrases, so they become 'so-oh' and 'de-si-yer'.
- Now tackle bars 18–26, adding the baritone part and then the alto part to the melody. To help each new part fit into the ensemble, get the other parts to hum their lines until singers are confident. Again, start slowly and speed up only once the singers are confident.
- Look at the melody for bars 26–37; the opening repeats in bars 26–9, but check the slight melody difference in bars 30–3.
- Add the baritone part for these bars, and note that the words have been turned into scat syllables, so keep them crisp and short.
- Now look at the alto part. Here it shadows the melody then breaks out into a solo 'lick'; make sure the singers distinguish the two by the style in their voices—light for the lick.
- Put all three parts together slowly, and check bars 34–5 for tuning.
- Move on to bars 38–53, where the baritones sing the melody. This time add in the alto part first, and then add the soprano. Make sure the altos and baritones don't sing through the rests—the soprano 'be do bop bop' needs to be clearly heard.
- Bars 54–64 are a contrast in style, and need to be smooth and soft in the soprano and baritone parts so that the alto part (optional solo) comes through the texture. Practise the 'oo' with forward pushed lips to make a vibrant and lively sound. Take care to avoid 'oo' becoming 'ah'.
- The final section (from bar 64) is a repeat of bars 26–37 shifted up a semitone. If singers find it hard to find the new notes, and can't pick them out from the accompaniment, then get them to sing bars 61–4 several times, raising the index fingers of both hands at bar 63 to help them with the upward shift.

Listen out

- Is the choral sound very light and rhythmic with a bright tone? Check it's not too 'plummy' and full-toned.
- Are the singers observing all the rests? Make sure that the notes in all parts are articulated separately to avoid a mushy sound when everyone is singing. The scat syllables should sound very percussive, and singers should breathe a few beats in advance of each phrase.

- What is the ensemble like? Check the balance between parts—the part singing the melody in each section should be slightly prominent. A good trick is for those singing the tune to raise their hands when they have it, so that they know when to sing out, and when to sing more gently to accompany the others.

Performing

- This piece demands bags of energy and attitude. It should be a sunny and cheerful performance. Keep an eye on the dynamics, as it requires some light and shade to make the music interesting.
- There are two optional solos in this song (bars 2–17 and 54–60). Introducing these could add some variety to the texture.
- If your choir likes choreography, this song lends itself to movement; try some simple sidesteps and finger clicks, perhaps stopping for bars 18–26 and 54–62.
- The backing CD presents a fuller accompaniment for this song to liven up performances.

23 My boy lollipop

Morris Levy, Johnny Roberts, and Robert Spencer
arr. Rebecca Berkley

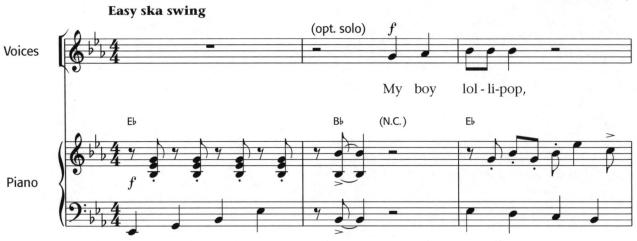

Ha, ho, my boy lol-li-pop,   ne-ver ev - er leave_ me,

be-cause   it would grieve   me;   my heart told me so._____

(end solo)

S.
I love you, I love you, I love you so;_   that I want you to

A.
I love you, I love you, I love you so;_   that I want you to

Bar.
I love you, I love you, I love you so;____

know.— I need you, I need you, I need you so,— and I'll ne-ver let you

know.— I need you, I need you, I need you so,— and I'll ne-ver let you

I need you, I need you, I need you so,— and I'll ne-ver let you

Eb7　　　Ab　　　Bb7 (N.C.)

mf cresc.

go.— My boy lol-li-pop, you make my heart go gid-dy up.

go.— My boy lol-li-pop, be do bop bop, you make my heart go gid-dy up, be do bop bop.

go.— Oh lol-li, ma lol-li-pop, do be ma lol-li, ma lol-li-pop,

Eb　　　Ab　　Bb9　　Eb

be do bop bop,   be my lol-li - pop,   be do bop bop,

My boy lol-li-pop,   you make my heart go gid-dy up.

My boy lol-li-pop,   you make my heart go gid-dy up.

be my lol-li - pop,   be do bop bop, you're my su - gar dan - dy.

You are as sweet as can - dy,   you're my su - gar dan - dy.

You are as sweet as can - dy,   you're my su - gar dan - dy.

be do bop bop,   be my lol-li - pop,   be do bop bop,

Ha, ho,   my boy lol-li-pop,   ne-ver ev - er leave_ me,

Ha, ho,   my boy lol-li-pop,   ne-ver ev - er leave_ me,

be my lol-li - pop,   my heart told me   so._

be-cause it would grieve   me;   my heart told me   so._

be-cause it would grieve   me;   my heart told me   so._

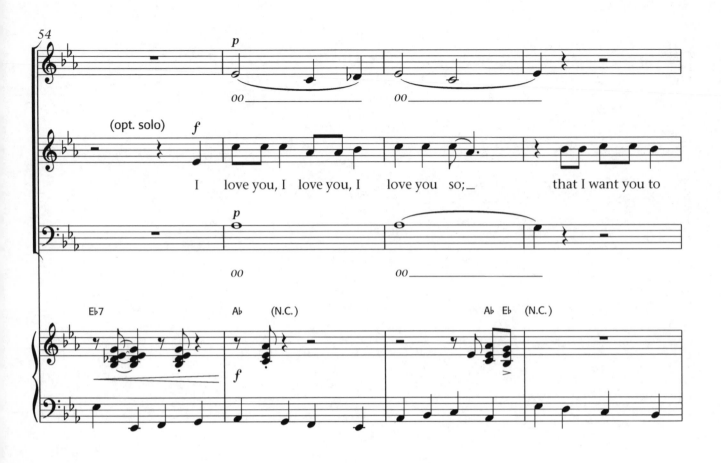

23 My boy lollipop

Vocal score

Morris Levy, Johnny Roberts, and Robert Spencer
arr. Rebecca Berkley

Easy ska swing

My boy lol-li-pop, you make my heart go

gid-dy up._ You are as sweet as can - dy, you're my su-gar_ dan-

- dy. Ha, ho, my boy lol-li-pop, ne-ver ev - er leave_ me,

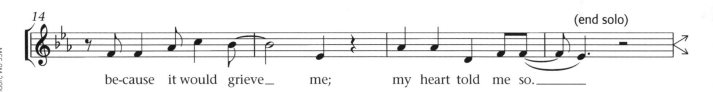

be-cause it would grieve_ me; my heart told me so._____

S.
I love you, I love you, I love you so;_ that I want you to

A.
I love you, I love you, I love you so;_ that I want you to

Bar.
I love you, I love you, I love you so;____

This page may be photocopied

This page may be photocopied

© 1957 EMI Longitude Music. This arrangement © 2009 EMI Longitude Music, EMI Music Publishing Ltd, London, W8 5SW

This page may be photocopied

Copyright Acknowledgements

▣ CD credits

Vocal tracks

Singers: Marion Ackrill, Gary Allen, Rebecca Berkley, Toby Blundell, Robyn Carpenter, James Goddard, Miriam Higgins, Victoria Hodges, Benjamin Lee, Simon Mead, Eleanor Moore, Flora Nicoll, Rosemary Nixon, Ben Tomlin, Ilana Yeshayahoo.
Soloist: Dennis Seaton (Song nos. 9, 11, 20, 21)
Keyboard: Philip Croydon
Drums: James Gafford (Song nos. 11, 18, 19, 20, 21, 22, 23)
Directed by Peter Hunt and recorded at St Matthew's Church, Southcote, Reading, by Mike McMillan.

Backing tracks

Song nos. 4, 10, 11, 20, 21, 22, 23
Bass guitar: Ben Atkins
Drums/percussion: Jon Buxton
Guitar: Pete Vecchietti
Keyboard: Rachael Claridge
Backings (band arrangements) by Pete Vecchietti and recorded at Ark T Studios by Jon Fletcher.

Song nos. 5, 16, and 17
Keyboard: Rachael Claridge (No. 5), David Blackwell (Nos. 16, 17)
Drums/percussion: Jon Buxton
Recorded at Ark T Studios by Jon Fletcher.

Song nos. 1, 2, 3, 6, 7, 8, 9, 12, 13, 14, 15
Keyboard: David Blackwell
Recorded at Ark T Studios by Jon Fletcher.

The Happy Smilers Mento Band

CD2 tracks 23, 24, 25, 26
Traditional performances of 'Brown Girl in the Ring', 'Fan me soldier man', 'Jane an' Louisa', and 'Mango Walk' by The Happy Smilers Mento Band.
Vocals and banjo: Neville Chambers
Guitar: Robin Plunkett
Rumba box: John Morgan
Recorded at World of Music Production Services, Ocho Rios, Jamaica, West Indies, by B. O'Hare.

Glossary

a cappella: unaccompanied singing

Aeolian mode: a scale (created by playing the white notes on a piano starting on A)

arpeggio: Italian term for a 'broken chord'—a collection of notes each sounded separately

call and response: sung phrases shared between a leader and a group; originally from field and work songs in Africa

canon (also round): a line of music which can be sung against itself, starting at different points within the phrase

chord: group of notes sounding at the same time

counter-melody: melody or tune which is different in nature from the main melody

crescendo: Italian term meaning 'growing' and used to indicate a gradual increase in sound level

decrescendo/diminuendo: Italian terms used to indicate gradually getting quieter

dynamics: indication of different levels of sound or volume

diatonic: notes of the scale which belong in the key (not chromatic notes)

ensemble: a group of performers; sounding together as one voice

imitation: where one part copies another

legato: smooth

lick: short repeated melodic fragment

mazurka: a dance of Polish origin which is played and danced with a strong accent on the first beat of each bar

mento: the Jamaican national dance song, equivalent to the 'merengue' from the Dominican Republic and the 'calypso' from Trinidad and Tobago. A fusion of African and European styles. Words explore social and local issues.

mixed voices: more than one voice type singing together (e.g. soprano and baritone)

ostinato: short repetitive rhythmic pattern

part-singing: different vocal lines sung at the same time **phrase**: line of music that is sung in one breath; notes that should be connected together to make musical sense (like a spoken sentence, punctuated by commas and full stops)

quadrille: a set of dances of European origin played at celebratory occasions in the plantation owner's house. The set consists of five dances in duple or triple metre.

reggae: 1960s style from Jamaica blending ska and rock steady; rhythmic style that accents the off beats. Strong lyrics that deal with religion, love, peace, poverty, injustice, and issues of politics and social injustice.

riff: jazz term for a short repetitive melodic pattern that is not improvised

round: *see* 'canon'

rote: learning of music (by ear) by repetition until secure

scat: from jazz; nonsense words and made-up syllables used for singing

ska: 1960s style of music combining mento and rhythm and blues; characterized by a walking bass-line

staccato: Italian term meaning 'detached'; notes should be shortened with gaps between them

syncopation: accenting or stressing weak beats in rhythm, to produce catchy rhythms; it cuts across the crotchet beat underlying the melody.

upbeat: short or quick note—often at the start of a phrase—which is sung just before the first or main beat of a bar

unison: when all parts sing the same tune together. Rhythmic unison is when the parts have the same rhythm together but not necessarily the same notes.